WHAT PARENTS NEED TO KNOW ABOUT DATING VIOLENCE

BARRIE LEVY

AND

PATRICIA OCCHIUZZO GIGGANS

D1303318

SEAL PRESS

To our children and grandchildren . . .
Ally, Chris, Ruby, Nisa, Johanna and Jedd
and their children . . .
and a vision of the future free from violence

306.73
L66Ew

Design by Clare Conrad

Library of Congress Cataloging-in-Publication Data

Levy, Barrie.
    What parents need to know about dating violence / Barrie Levy and Patricia Occhiuzzo Giggans.
        1. Dating violence. 2. Dating violence—Prevention.
I. Giggans, Patricia Occhiuzzo. II. Title.
HQ801.83.L49   1995   306.73—dc20   94-42614
ISBN: 1-878067-47-8

Printed in the United States of America
First printing, June 1995
10 9 8 7 6 5 4 3 2 1

Distributed to the trade by Publishers Group West
In Canada: Publishers Group West Canada, Toronto, Ontario
In the U.K. and Europe: Airlift Book Company, London, England

ACKNOWLEDGMENTS

This book reflects the generosity of many people who shared the stories of their experiences so that others might learn from them. Teens and parents participated in hours of interviews as they described relationship violence and how it affected them and their families. We are grateful that they trusted us with the task of telling their stories. To respect their privacy, we will not name them individually, but we acknowledge our appreciation for their important contribution to this project.

We thank the following people for their assistance and support. Cheryl Majka, from Rainbow Battered Women's Services and Francine Ocon, from the L.A. Commission on Assaults Against Women (LACAAW) were instrumental in introducing us to parents and teens who were interested in being interviewed. Lydia Bodin, L.A. County Deputy District Attorney took the time to review our legal information. Gena Philibert-Ortega's work with teens has inspired ideas for this book.

Our publishers at Seal Press were enthusiastic about this project from its beginning. We especially want to thank Faith Conlon, our editor, who nurtured this book from idea to reality, and copy editor Martin Cobb, who made helpful suggestions for its improvement.

Linda Garnets was our constant editor, problem-solver, cook and coach. Ellen Ledley's thoughtfulness and experience in the field of domestic violence were invaluable. Linda and Ellen provided feedback, encouragement through the hard parts and celebrations when deadlines were met. Ally Giggans and Johanna Johnston transcribed and typed, and Johanna calmed us as she tackled the computer for us. Elise Asch lent her meticulous eye for proofreading.

Patti thanks the staff and Board of Directors of LACAAW for their support, especially Leah Aldridge for her energy and Cathy Friedman for her stamina. She acknowledges the importance of Wednesday Night Family Support Group, and discussions with Veronica Villalobos, Chris Giggans and their friends for adding perspectives of teenagers to her work.

Lastly we want to acknowledge the respect we have for our children who, as teenagers, challenged us and taught us to be better parents.

CONTENTS

PREFACE

In the eight years since the death of my daughter, Jenny, the issue of teen dating violence has virtually exploded in the media. We now have curricula in schools, programs on television, articles in magazines and books to provide information and guidance. This book is an important addition to Barrie Levy's two previous works: *Dating Violence: Young Women in Danger*, which provided guidance to counselors and others who work closely with teens, and *In Love and In Danger*, which targeted teens themselves. This book, by targeting parents, may well be the crucial key in the effort to save our children.

As I remember my last year with Jenny, I remember my absolute ignorance of the existence of teen dating violence both as a new phenomenon in our society and as a reality in my own daughter's life. Because I was so unaware of these problems, I didn't know enough to even ask questions, let alone to provide my support and offer Jenny the help she so desperately needed. How I wish a book such as this had been available in 1986.

Had I been afforded an opportunity to learn of the warning signs and patterns of abuse, I believe I would have been alerted to what was going on in Jenny's life. The patterns of abuse in Jenny's relationship were, in hindsight, so predictable. Her boyfriend attempted to control her through isolation from family and friends, intimidation using physical abuse, and manipulation through guilt and other emotional game-playing. Finally he used violence to silence and control her forever.

Recently my husband and I visited Mark, Jenny's killer. As participants in a new program called the "Victim-Offender Reconciliation Program," we were able to go into the prison and visit with Mark for nearly four hours. It was a painful and enlightening meeting. I learned that Jenny was "expendable," that any young woman could have been the object of Mark's wrath, could have lost her life, if the same set of circumstances had been present. A painful reality: Jenny was not special to Mark. She was just the object of his control, the wrong person in the wrong place at the wrong time.

I noticed that Mark used the word "control" at least fifty times during our conversation. His need to control Jenny and every aspect of her life was chillingly apparent as he spoke. His explanation for going to our home the day he killed Jenny? "I had to get control of the situation." When I pointed out that his actions had sent him to a place where he lost all control over his life, he responded, "But they can't control my mind." My belief is that because these battering young men have had no control over their own lives during childhood, due to abuse, alcoholism, poverty, etc., they therefore must have absolute control over their girlfriends as a means of feeling powerful.

It is possible that you, the reader, have picked up this book because you have a flickering suspicion that your child may be involved in a violent relationship. Perhaps you saw a television show which focused on this issue and you experienced a moment of cold fear because the discussion was too familiar, too close to home. I applaud you for your decision to buy this book. Doing nothing is the worst thing you can do! I encourage you to read this book and discuss the things you learn with your child. Despite their attempts to make us believe otherwise, our children need us to guide and protect them. Jenny didn't tell me what was happening to her and I didn't know enough to ask. Don't let this happen to you and your child. Don't let another day go by where you simply wonder and worry, but take no action. Please read the suggestions in this book and consider using them.

My family has suffered a devastating loss. We live with sadness every day. Perhaps it could have been prevented if we had only been educated. I hope this book will save other lives, that there will be no more Jenny's.

Vicki Crompton
December 1994

Vicki Crompton of Davenport, Iowa, authored the chapter "A Parent's Story" in the first book of this series, Dating Violence: Young Women in Danger. *Vicki's daughter, Jenny, died when her ex-boyfriend stalked her, broke into her home, and killed her. Jenny Crompton was fifteen years old.*

INTRODUCTION

You, a parent, are often the last to know about the real life of your teenager. That is why we have written this book. We receive calls from parents seeking advice about getting their teenagers out of battering relationships. We talk to teens who are in pain and in danger, but won't ask a parent or another adult for help. Teens usually don't talk honestly to their parents about their experiences, and parents who find out are worn out from trying to figure out what to do. The most powerful realization for us was that teens need their parents—violence is too serious for them to confront and handle on their own. Our work with teens in classrooms, in counseling and in groups has confirmed for us that parents' involvement is critical, and that parents need support to be effective.

Adolescence

Parenting teens is challenging even at its easiest because of the enormous changes and growth that take place during adolescence.

Adolescence is an important stage in the development of an individual's identity. Children make the transition to adulthood as they explore who they are: things they like and do well, what they want to be, their attitudes and values, their sexuality, and how they see themselves as women and men.

In distinguishing their individuality in relation to adults, adolescents conform to peer norms. They prioritize their relationships with their friends over those with their families. Peer pressure can be intense. The fear of being different or ostracized can create rigid conformity; if the adolescent doesn't conform, he or she may experience a great deal of stress.

The pressures and vulnerability that characterize this stage of development make battering in teen relationships unique and very different from domestic violence involving adults.

Adolescent girls and boys may not yet have the flexibility to be themselves. Feeling the pressure to prove they are not "too attached" to their families may lead them to behave like exaggerated adults. Definitions of "normal" masculine or feminine behavior often follow stereotyped patterns of dominance and passivity: the girl's caretaking role, her responsibility for the success of the relationship, her social dependence on her boyfriend, and the boy's insistence on having his girlfriend's attention on demand. The expectations of a girlfriend, especially from her boyfriend, may pressure her to give up activities, talents and other relationships, making her boyfriend the priority. The expectations of a boyfriend, especially from his friends, often pressure him to be sexually aggressive, to make all the decisions in a relationship, and to dominate and control his girlfriend's activities and behavior. The social demands of adolescence often include the pressure to have a boyfriend or girlfriend and to have sex.

Teens are inexperienced in relationships. Therefore, they have difficulty managing the complex feelings, decisions and conflicts that arise. Teens romanticize love and relationships. They often interpret jealousy, possessiveness and abuse as signs of love. This makes teens vulnerable because they do not instinctively define abuse as a problem.

During adolescence, teens' relationships with their parents change. As teens gain more independence, they are afraid of parental interference undermining their newly found freedom.

It becomes important to them to not need their parents. They expect parents to be critical, punishing and restrictive. They experience conflicts with parents over their autonomy, power and control.

Teens have private aspects of their lives, and feelings and experiences they don't want to share. The difference between privacy and secrecy can be confusing at this stage. The problem with maintaining a secret, as opposed to privacy, is that the teen feels ashamed and may feel torn about telling a parent. Parents have difficulty distinguishing between their teen's right to privacy and the parent's need to know. This issue is intensified when the secret in question has to do with violence or abuse.

There are multiple areas of challenge, conflict and stress in the lives of teens. They make daily decisions about drugs, alcohol, sex, school and work. They are affected by issues of violence, AIDS, pregnancy, gangs, and ethnic conflict and racism. They are under pressure to be successful in school and to plan for the future. Coping with a violent dating relationship takes place in a complex context of multiple problems that are a natural part of adolescence, and which complicate the communication and trust between parents and teens.

Dating violence affects both boys and girls. Both boys and girls have been victimized in intimate relationships, and both boys and girls have perpetrated abuse. However, the overwhelming majority of cases involve a male batterer and a female victim. Throughout our text we refer to batterers as "he" and victims as "she," reflecting the majority of cases, and simplifying the language. We do not want readers to ignore that violence can be inflicted by either partner in any relationship, by males upon females, males upon males, females upon males and females upon females. In this book we generally address the reader as a parent of a daughter who is being battered.

Guidelines for Parents

As parents ourselves, we know how hard it is to convince teens that they need us and that they can trust us to help them. We also know how hard it is to resist the urge to take charge and fix their problems, or to give up completely.

We don't know of any one way to "fix" the problem of violence in a relationship. We can share with you some of the efforts parents we know have made and how well they have worked. More importantly, we can tell you about several guidelines that we have found helpful.

When parents approach us, it usually becomes clear that they have one primary goal: "Get my child away from this abuser!" As we talk about the realities and the factors they are dealing with, parents ultimately realize that the problem is complex and changing from moment to moment. Effectively dealing with a battering relationship is a *process* that requires flexibility, especially in setting priorities.

When you first discover that your teenager has been beaten up by a boyfriend or a girlfriend, you may be tempted to take dramatic steps to get the batterer out of your teen's life. It is natural to feel so outraged and fearful for your teen's safety that you want to stop the beating and protect your teen immediately. Ideally, you can have that kind of impact. But usually immediate, dramatic steps only work when the victim is actively or passively ready to participate in getting away from the abuser.

There are many other ways in which you can be effective in dealing with the battering when you cannot help end the relationship. You do not want to neglect the variety of needs or opportunities to help your teen. You do not want to cut off contact with your teen, which will leave her more isolated and vulnerable. Another frequent outcome of an inflexible approach to the problem is that the teen feels further victimized, helpless, overwhelmed, unable to take steps on her own behalf, trapped in the relationship, or forced to collude with the batterer against her parents. Parents' actions may reinforce the batterer's powerful message that the victim is the problem.

Recognizing your intervention as a process rather than a single action is the only realistic way to respond to a complex, changeable situation that requires careful and flexible decision-making. There are different phases, from your suspicion to discovering there really is violence to repeated incidents of violence, along with the victim's push/pull reactions. Each phase requires different types of actions on your part.

There are usually several priorities, all of them high, competing for your attention at once. On reflection, you may realize that you have several goals. You want to end the battering and/or the battering relationship. You want to help your teen be as safe as possible, to take care of her own safety, and to become free of the hold the batterer has over her. You want to stop the physical violence and threats that cause you to fear your teen will be injured or killed. You want to reduce the damaging effects of the battering relationship on your family life. You want to heal and recover from the effects of violence. You probably have other goals that are specific to your particular situation.

To be effective, it is important to be aware of ways to empower your teen when you are deciding how to intervene. This involves participating with your teen in the process of dealing with the violence, helping her to see what is really going on and to make the best decisions she can. By empowering your teen, you are helping her to build strengths in all aspects of her life so she can be as strong as possible in resisting the abuse. You do not want to ignore the aspects of her life that are working well in spite of the violence. It is more effective to build strengths and supports rather than to focus constantly on the relationship. Ultimately, what you want your teen to accomplish is to be free of the grip the relationship has on her, to focus less on the relationship and more on the other aspects of her life.

We have found that parents often get caught up in power struggles with their teens. Dealing with teen dating violence means dealing with conflicts over power and control—in the battering relationship and in the parent/child relationship. Parents quickly find out that attempts to control their teens are fruitless, and generally escalate the conflict without solving the problem. The teen who is being battered may find herself in a battle between her abuser and her parents, with no safe place to think for herself.

Fear of violence can lead to impulsive, dramatic overreactions, which undermine your effectiveness. Quiet, positive action is as important and powerful as intervention that involves major decisions or lots of activity. Observing, gathering information, quietly communicating about your concerns can have an important impact or can prepare you for difficult decisions that arise later.

Maintaining open communication may provide your teen with a lifeline that keeps her safe. The secrecy involved in battering relationships and parents' overreactions based on fear can result in little or no communication between parent and teen. An important principle of effective parenting in general, open communication is especially important when dealing with dating violence.

Setting limits, while sustaining a connection between you and your teen, gives her a supportive structure while she struggles with the tumultuous ups and downs of the violence. Setting limits involves being quietly firm, clear and realistic about the consequences and then following through. This is especially important as you determine your own limits regarding the impact of your daughter's relationship on you and your whole family.

Overview of this Book

The drama of teen dating violence has a large cast of characters. It is natural to focus on a victim and a perpetrator, but entire families are affected. It is estimated that almost a third of teens experience violence or abuse in a dating relationship. Violence during adolescence is often the first sign of the potential for repeated violence in adult relationships. We can see how the effects of violence multiply when we consider how many people are affected by each battering relationship, while it lasts and afterwards.

Studies have shown that teens rarely seek help from adults about this problem. Parents don't expect these kinds of problems with children of this age, and often don't recognize the violence for what it is. When not recognized and actively confronted, violence that starts at this critical stage of a young person's life may have damaging effects for years to come.

Clearly, parents need to know all they can about dating violence. The first section of the book describes what it is and alerts parents to the warning signs of a violent relationship. We have found that emotional, sexual and physical abuse are intertwined, and must be seen as having the same roots. We pay particular attention to sexual abuse as part of the battering relationship because it is the most difficult aspect of battering for teens to reveal and understand, and thus is often ignored or overlooked.

Everyone asks why a girl stays with a boyfriend who treats her badly. Parents torment themselves trying to understand why their teen puts up with mistreatment. This focus suggests that the girl is making it happen. More important is the question, why do some people hurt and batter someone they love? All it takes to be in a battering relationship is to fall in love with someone who is willing to use violence. Understanding why a person stays with a batterer can be helpful, not to blame them for the violence, but rather to understand how to help them make choices to better protect and take care of themselves. Ultimately, however, it is up to the batterer to stop the violence. This book discusses the complex combination of social and psychological factors that contribute to someone using violence in an intimate relationship, and the dynamics of the abuse that keep the victim in the relationship.

Parents have described the "rollercoaster" experience of coping with the many crises involved in their teen's violent relationship. The entire family suffers from tumultuous ups and downs as the victim goes back and forth about being in the relationship, and as the abuse quiets and escalates through the stages of the cycle of violence. We aim to help parents recognize the stresses and strains on their own relationship, on their other children and on the family as a whole.

After describing what dating violence is all about and how it affects you and your teen, we then provide guidelines for making decisions about how to intervene effectively. These guidelines represent common themes we have heard from parents, and involve recognizing the limits of parental control over teens and strengthening the parent/teen relationship.

To plan for their teen's safety, parents can advocate for and with their teen, using school systems and criminal justice systems. Information provided in this book aims to give parents ideas about how these systems can work for them. Safety planning is optimized when family, friends and neighbors are involved, as supporters and as extensions of the battered teen's safety net. The advocacy and safety issues change when the battered teen is breaking up with the batterer, so additional information is included to alert parents to ways to handle the increased risk of serious violence immediately after a break-up. Counseling to break free of violence and to recover from violence are very helpful to anyone who has been battered. Family counseling and supportive counseling for parents are also important resources for dealing with the multiple effects of dating violence. We include guidelines for selecting a counselor who specializes in domestic and dating violence.

We can't talk about families without talking about culture, values, beliefs and traditions. And we can't talk about taking action to confront dating violence without challenging traditional values and beliefs regarding the family, courtship and marriage, male/female relationships and seeking help. Cultures and ethnic and religious communities can provide valuable resources for coping and support. At the same time we suggest that it is often in the best interest of the teen to challenge cultural beliefs that make her safety and recovery from violence more difficult.

Values and beliefs also affect the response to violence in teen gay and lesbian relationships. Studies have shown that battering takes place as frequently in gay and lesbian relationships as in heterosexual relationships. However, negative attitudes and hostility towards homosexuality keep gay and lesbian teen relationships secret, and the violence hidden. This book affirms the need to recognize that these relationships exist, and that gay, lesbian and bisexual teens need parental support to overcome both homophobia and violence.

It is also important to recognize that batterers have families too. You may be reading this book because of your concern about a teen who is abusive. The families of violent and abusive teens are also affected by dating violence. A chapter written for the parents of abusers devotes much-needed attention to this issue, and describes ways that parents of teens who are abusive can make a difference in confronting dating violence.

Whether children have already been affected by violence or not, it is important to help them relate to people in non-violent ways. The best approach to preparing them to prevent interpersonal violence is to teach them to think about their own safety and to teach them skills that form the basis for healthy relationships. The appendices to this book include tools to be used in teaching teens these skills. Both boys and girls can learn assertive ways to communicate and solve problems without inappropriate aggression or passivity. We must not only talk with teens about guarding against violence, but we must also show them the characteristics of healthy relationships.

The information and ideas in this book have come from the many parents and teens who have shared their stories and advice with us. Throughout the book, their stories may inspire you, remind you that you are not alone or simply let you know about what other families have experienced. We hope they will remind you of your strengths and accomplishments as well as stimulate your thinking as you respond to the unique aspects of your family's situation.

Barrie Levy and Patricia Occhiuzzo Giggans
February 1995, Los Angeles, California

WHAT PARENTS NEED TO KNOW ABOUT DATING VIOLENCE

WHAT IS DATING VIOLENCE?

You may feel that yours is the only family that is having a problem with dating violence. But many teenagers have problems with violence in a relationship with a boyfriend or a girlfriend. Surveys of students in high schools and colleges all over the United States have led researchers to estimate that twenty-eight percent of the students experienced physical violence in a dating relationship.[1] Studies on date rape indicate that sixty-seven percent of young women reporting rape were assaulted in a dating situation.[2]

Dating violence happens everywhere and to all kinds of people. There is no particular culture or community in which it occurs or does not occur. The occurrence of dating violence has been documented in large cities and in small farming communities, in wealthy neighborhoods and in housing projects. It occurs in every culture and ethnic group. It happens in gay and lesbian as well as heterosexual relationships. It happens to teens who have babies and to those who do not. It happens to teens who live together, and to those who live with their parents.

Dating violence is *serious*. The potential for murder is present in every violent relationship. According to the FBI, twenty percent of homicide victims are between the ages of fifteen and twenty-four.[3] One out of every three women murdered in the United States is killed by a husband or a boyfriend.[4] Even an abusive boyfriend who does not intend to kill his girlfriend can accidentally kill her with hard shoves or threats with a weapon.

It is most common for the victim to be female and the violent partner to be male. Young men are also victims and young women are also violent. However, the great majority of abusers are young men, and their victims are young women. The social tolerance for boys to be aggressive towards girls seems to make it far more common for boys to be violent. Girls who victimize their boyfriends are more likely to be emotionally or verbally abusive and boys are more likely to use threats of or actual physical violence. Girls are less likely to inflict severe injuries; however, abuse inflicted by girls can be intimidating, and boys can be afraid to displease or to make their girlfriends angry.

Several studies have reported that young men are more violent when they begin to view themselves as part of a couple.[5] Often abusers become more violent when they think the relationship is going to end, or after their girlfriend or boyfriend breaks up with them. Thus, the chance of being seriously injured or killed becomes higher when the victim decides to break up the relationship. This makes breaking up frightening for the victim, who may try to break up (and then get back together) several times before actually ending the relationship.

Many of the victims of dating violence believe that their partner's violence is a sign of love. The violent partner seems to accept violence as a means to obtain a desired goal, for example to "frighten" or to "intimidate" or to "force the other person to give me something." Violence is seen as tolerable, or as normal, in dating relationships.

Teens don't use the term "dating" the way we do in this book. A more accurate term would be "courtship," but no one uses this term any more. Teens might call it "seeing," "going with" or "kicking it." We are talking about intimate (usually sexual) relationships in which two people see themselves as a couple with a potential future together.

In a violent intimate relationship, a person repeatedly (1) uses or threatens to use physical force against the other, (2) verbally attacks, demeans or humiliates the other to control her or him, and/or (3) forces or coerces the other to participate in sexual acts. It is *not* the same as getting angry or having a fight. It happens again and again, and one person is afraid of and intimidated by the other.

Controlling behavior is not always defined as battering or abuse. A teenage girl can be in a relationship with a boyfriend who is self-centered, controlling, frequently insists on his own way, or criticizes a lot. If confronted or told he can't have his way, he backs down. He may become angry, but he doesn't become explosive, violent, verbally attacking or threatening. His girlfriend is not afraid of him. There is some give and take in the relationship. He is not what we call a batterer. Some things he does could be called abusive, but his behavior does not fit the repeated cycle of violence that characterizes battering relationships. Defining this distinction can be difficult. Some controlling behavior, however, does have the potential for becoming abusive or violent.

In this book we use the terms "batterer" and "abuser," "battered teen" and "abused teen," and "violence" and "abuse" interchangeably. All of these terms refer to the full range of behavior that is emotionally, sexually and physically injurious.

As a parent, it is probably difficult for you to read details about the kinds of abuse teens can suffer in a battering relationship. It is horrifying to imagine that these things could happen to your child. We hope, as you read this book you will feel supported while you deal with some of the most difficult problems a parent with a teenager can face.

Emotional Abuse

If your daughter is being abused by a boyfriend, she is probably being emotionally abused whether or not he has been physically or sexually abusive toward her. Emotional abuse can be very confusing for teens. It is confusing to be constantly criticized, blamed for everything that goes wrong and humiliated in front of others—by the same person who expresses intense love. Emotional abuse also causes wounds such as self-doubt, self-hatred, shame, feelings of going crazy, or feeling unable to survive without the abuser. These wounds are invisible to others, unlike the wounds caused by physical violence, which are more easily recognized as hurtful and wrong. So, as a result of emotional abuse your daughter may feel that she caused her own injuries, and that she is the cause of the problems in her relationship.

Emotional abuse is especially damaging because it is not always done in anger. It is often done in the guise of love, and accompanied by confusing expressions of caring. "It's a good thing you have me to love you, because you are so [ugly, crazy, disgusting . . .], no one else would want you." "I'm only telling you that you dress like a whore because I love you." "We have each other; we don't need anyone else. Your friends and parents are trying to keep us apart. No one else understands us and what we have together."

Jealousy and possessiveness that control and restrict the other's behavior can be emotionally abusive. The abuser's jealousy and suspiciousness may lead to accusations, explosive outbursts and name-calling, interrogations about everything his victim does or says. Your daughter's jealous boyfriend may check up on her. He may follow her or have friends follow her. He may call her many times each day, and explode if she is not there to answer the phone. He may go through her things checking for "clues" of her "infidelity." He may call or find her when she is at work or at school or spending time with others and demand her attention (for example, by having something urgent he wants her to do for him).

Her boyfriend's jealousy and explosive temper can make it too frightening for your daughter to do anything that might set him off. So she gradually stops doing things outside the relationship. Sixteen-year-old Jim's girlfriend was terrified of his raging fits when he was jealous. Jim didn't hit her. He yelled at her, called her names, interrogated her for hours about everything she said or did with anybody, going over and over the same answers to his questions and accusations. Later, when seeing a counselor, Jim said, "After a while, I got what I wanted: complete control over my girlfriend. Power."

Threats of suicide or violence are emotionally abusive. Your daughter's boyfriend may become seriously depressed, especially if he is afraid of losing her, and he may feel like killing or hurting himself. This can be terrifying for his girlfriend. Imagine feeling that you could cause someone you love to kill himself! However, his threats to kill himself may also be a way of emotionally controlling her. Rather than getting the help he needs, or turning to others for support, he wants only his girlfriend to drop everything and take care of him. Or he may threaten to kill her or her family if she ever leaves him. This has the same effects of terrifying and trapping her.

Isolation also results from emotional abuse. Abusers get control by keeping their girlfriend or boyfriend isolated. Your daughter's abusive boyfriend may tell her that her friends and family are no good. He may have a fit of rage every time she sees a friend, or he may accuse her of betraying him if she talks about him to anyone else. He may try to get her to see her family as the "enemy" of their relationship, and to feel that talking to you, her parents, makes her "disloyal" to him.

Physical Abuse

Physical abuse is rarely a one-time incident, but is part of a pattern in an abusive relationship. The violence or the threat of violence happens again and again. Physical abuse is used to control, to restrict, to intimidate and frighten. It is generally accompanied by verbal and emotional abuse. The violence generally escalates, becoming more severe over time. Even if the physical violence does not occur frequently, the abuser may use frequent threats of violence after it has happened once.

Physical abuse can be lethal, accidentally or deliberately causing death. Physical abuse includes pushing, hitting, slapping, kicking, beating with a fist, choking, and attacking with an object or a weapon. Some teens have been restrained hard enough to cause bruises, or pinned down, or pulled by the hair. Often batterers deliberately inflict injuries in places on the body that don't show. We have talked with teens who have been seriously or permanently injured, such as one young woman who lost an eye, another who lost her hearing, and others who were shot or stabbed.

Your daughter may have been slapped so hard that handprints remained on her face. She may have been choked until she passed out, and you could see the red marks on her neck. She may have been shoved or thrown across the room, causing a concussion when she hit a wall or a table.

Sexual Abuse

Sexual abuse is mistreatment by sexual acts, demands or insults. Your daughter may have been violently forced to have sex, or she may have been coerced or manipulated into having sex. She has been "coerced" if she has been afraid to say no because she is afraid of being rejected, humiliated or beaten—acts which, if committed within a relationship, are as illegal as when committed by a stranger.

Your daughter may have been forced to perform sexual acts she did not want to do, or that were intended to humiliate or degrade her. She may have been told lies about what is "normal" sex, or what "guys need," or how girls are supposed to act in bed. She may never have felt anything but pain during sex in a relationship of months or years.

Some girls have reported that they have been forced to have sex with others, or to watch their boyfriends have sex with someone else. Some have been humiliated or insulted sexually, or made to feel disgusting or ugly. Many have been forced to have sex without protection from pregnancy or AIDS. Some girls have been raped vaginally or anally or forced to have oral sex with their boyfriend. Teens have described other kinds of sexual abuse: being tied up; having breasts or genitalia cut, bitten or mutilated; being stripped and stared at for long periods of time; and being forced to watch or enact scenes from pornographic films.

When asked "What are some of the ways you have been *emotionally abused*?" teens answered:

- yelled at
- constantly blamed for partner's own faults
- verbally harassed
- called names
- money stolen
- constantly accused of flirting with others
- publicly humiliated
- possessions broken

When asked "What are some of the ways you have been *physically abused*?" teens answered:

- scratched
- arm twisted
- choked
- beaten up
- hair pulled
- burned
- slapped
- arm held so tight it bruised
- head hit against wall
- dumped out of car
- cut with knife
- knocked down
- hit with object
- punched in face

When asked "What are some of the ways you have been *sexually abused*?" teens answered:

- called sexual names
- boyfriend threatened to get a new woman
- boyfriend wanted sex after hitting
- forced to have sex
- raped
- forced to do disgusting sex acts
- boyfriend always wanted sex, mad when I didn't want to
- slapped, pinched to get his way
- forced to have sex without protection
- bitten, breast pinched

The Cycle of Violence

> One small disagreement would lead to another. . . . [It] would
> build to a crescendo, which always ended with . . . Mike's vio-
> lence. Then the storm would clear, and we would make up
> passionately and be blissfully happy for days or weeks until
> the next storm started to build. — Marge, 18

You may have noticed that there is a pattern, a cycle in
your daughter's relationship. Abusers seem to be like two
different people: loving some of the time, and cruel some of
the time. Their behavior and mood go back and forth in repeated cycles. As time passes, the cycles get shorter and
shorter. For many abusers, the *honeymoon* or *making up* stage
eventually stops, and they go back and forth between *tension-building* and *explosion.*

Dana and Jason are both sixteen years old. They go to the
same high school. They have been going together for eight
months, and going through the stages in the cycle of violence.
Their experience is typical of abusive dating relationships.

The Tension-Building Stage

During the *tension-building* stage, Jason becomes more and
more temperamental, edgy, critical and explosive. He blows
up easily, throws things, constantly criticizes Dana. He "pun-
ishes" her for her "mistakes." He blames her for anything he
feels is wrong—no matter what she does.

Jason is jealous and possessive. He accuses Dana of dressing too sexily, or flirting, or having sex with others. He calls
her constantly to find out where she is—or to make sure she
doesn't go anywhere.

Sometimes, Dana thinks Jason's demands are flattering.
They seem to prove his love. She knows she is important to
him. But little by little, Dana has become more and more afraid

of doing something that will trigger his temper.

During this tension-building stage, Dana tries to be very careful. She is afraid to do anything she believes will make Jason become violent. To keep the peace, she tries to please him. When he wants to know where she's been, she attempts to tell him the truth. Then she tells him what she thinks he wants to hear. When he gets mad at what she says, she explains.

After a while she realizes it doesn't matter what she says. Jason twists whatever she says and just gets angrier and angrier. Sometimes when he wants to have sex it isn't enjoyable for Dana because he's rough with her. When she tries to calm him down or humor him, or she becomes quiet just to get it over with, his anger keeps building and the tension increases.

Dana becomes tense and nervous. She gets terrible stomach aches; her doctor thinks she is developing an ulcer. Sometimes she gets sick. She is usually a happy person, full of energy, but when the tension between her and Jason gets bad, she becomes withdrawn and depressed. She watches Jason closely but forgets to take care of herself, and goes to school in her oldest or dirtiest clothes. She becomes so distracted with worry about Jason that she can't concentrate in school, and although she is usually a good student, she forgets assignments and fails exams.

Dana's mom, Peggy, notices the changes in her daughter's behavior. She sees that Dana doesn't care about school or about her appearance. Dana *used* to spend hours in front of the bathroom mirror! She notices that Dana is jumpy, quick to answer the phone when it rings and ready to drop anything if Jason insists. She also realizes that Dana apologizes for everything and criticizes herself a lot. When Peggy asks

Dana what is wrong, Dana either says "Nothing" or jumps all over her ("Why do you always think something is wrong?!"). Peggy tells Dana, "I'm worried about you. You're upset all the time, and you've never done this badly in school." Dana bursts into tears, saying she has too much on her mind. In the next few days, she fluctuates between telling her mother what is happening and protecting Jason, blaming herself. She keeps telling her mother not to worry, that everything will be fine again soon.

Jason's mom, Suzanne, can also feel the tension when Jason is around. He responds with short, nasty answers to her questions, and he is quick to blow up at his little brother. A few minutes later he apologizes and smiles as if nothing has happened. She overhears Jason talking with Dana on the phone and being cruel to and critical of her. When she comments to Jason that he isn't being nice to Dana, Jason yells at her to mind her own business. Suzanne is intimidated by him, but cautions him, "Be careful because you know what a bad temper you have."

The Explosion Stage

The tension-building stage usually ends with a violent *explosion*. The abuser verbally, physically and/or sexually attacks the victim. Generally the attack is more severe than the abuse inflicted during the tension-building stage, and worse than previous explosions.

Jason's anger builds, and he stops trying to cool off. Dana tries to get away from Jason each time before he explodes; sometimes she can, and other times she can't. Jason loses control and lashes out at Dana. He calls her names, hits her, forces her to have sex, and won't let her get away from him. He feels enraged, and wants to humiliate and hurt her.

Then his rage subsides and it's over—until the next time. Afterwards he always feels sorry, and is afraid that Dana will leave him. He has given her a black eye and bruises. She can't stand for him to touch her. When he sees how he has hurt her, he cries, and begs her to forgive him.

Dana realizes that she has been fooling herself by thinking (again) that Jason will ever stop his violence. It's a relief for her too when it's over, but it also makes her angry. No matter what she does, Jason hurts her. A couple of times, she has broken up with him after he has beaten her up.

Peggy and her husband, Don, are terrified because this time Jason has really hurt their daughter. Until now, they had not known that he beats her. They are afraid Dana will make excuses for him, forgive him and get back together with him. Peggy and Don talk with Dana about getting away from Jason and getting her life together without him. Peggy is also worried about Don. He is furious with Jason, and threatens to "take matters in his own hands." Peggy and Dana are afraid Don will get hurt or make things worse. They file a police report, and try to convince Don to let the police handle Jason. Everyone is relieved that Dana is no longer covering up for Jason.

Suzanne knows that Jason has a real problem, but she can't believe that her son would hurt Dana so badly without provocation. When Jason says that Dana pushed him, and that it was her fault, Suzanne wants to believe him. She feels powerless to do anything about Jason's violence, and hopes that the police report will have some effect on him.

The Making Up Stage

The third stage, the *honeymoon* or *making up* stage that follows the explosion, is what keeps the couple together. Jason is apologetic, romantic, passionate. He promises he will change and never hurt her again. Dana still feels afraid and vulnerable, and wants to get away from him. But he is so much like his old self, and he feels so bad, that she begins to remember the things she loves about him when he is not violent. She knows he loves her and needs her.

They become loving again, and Jason is not so tense, but fun to be with again. Dana feels better, relieved, and her energy is restored. Jason doesn't feel so easily irritated and jealous, and doesn't seem to twist everything Dana says or does anymore. They go to their special places and enjoy their time together. Another honeymoon stage is under way.

They both find excuses for his "blow-up"—his unhappy childhood, his failures in school, her failure to keep him happy. They may even think that his violence was justified or her bruises deserved. They deny the fact that the violence is Jason's problem. They both begin to believe that the violence was a "misunderstanding" and won't happen again . . . until the tension begins to build. . . .

Peggy and Don watch Dana avoid them and spend all of her time with Jason again. They can't believe that Dana has forgotten her bruises so quickly and that she seems to think he won't be violent again. When they talk to her about Jason she defends him, makes excuses for him and gets angry with them for trying to interfere in the one thing in her life that makes her happy. They also know that Dana does not let them know about her problems with Jason until they get really bad. The honeymoon stage for Jason and Dana is full of tension for Peggy and Don.

Suzanne keeps hoping that this time Jason will realize his violence causes serious problems. She is relieved that he is his old self again. She worries about Dana, that she keeps going back to him.

Suzanne's, Don's and Peggy's worries are justified. Generally, the cycle of violence continues to be repeated, and becomes worse unless the person who is violent takes active steps to change or the victim leaves the relationship.

2

RECOGNIZING
THE WARNING SIGNS

Parents have varying experiences of finding out about their daughter's or son's abuse or abusiveness. Some find out as soon as the abuse starts—they see the bruises, witness the verbal or physical attack, or their child tells them. Others don't find out until the violence has become so severe they are notified of it by the school, a hospital or the police. Still others don't find out until after the relationship has ended.

But there are a number of warning signs that can help parents recognize if their child is being abused. The following refers to an abused daughter, but it could be a son.

Signs of Abuse

Does your daughter come home with injuries she can't explain?

Bruises, red marks (as from a slap), a limp, clumps of hair missing, torn clothes, burn or choke marks: these are visible signs of physical violence. Often the teen's explanation doesn't match the injury. The second or third time, it is no longer plausible. You may find out when you ask enough times, and your daughter gives up trying to cover up the truth.

> My daughter is athletic, so she'd tell me that she had been injured when playing soccer. She didn't used to get so many injuries, and she never had so many soccer games either. Finally, I confronted her, and asked "What is going on? Is Todd hitting you?" She denied it at first, but then she couldn't explain how a soccer ball could have given her a red mark around her neck. She finally told me that Todd had choked her to keep her from leaving his house. This had been going on for months. — Pamela, mother of Sara, 16

Do you see signs that she is afraid of her boyfriend?

> She went to the market with me the other day, and she began rushing me through the checkout line. She said she had to get home to be there for Eddie's call. She seemed to be afraid. I rushed with her and didn't say anything. The phone rang as soon as we walked in the door. I heard her explaining, apologizing, trying to calm him down, telling him, "Don't come over here! My mom's here." After she hung up, we had a long talk. That's when she told me that Eddie keeps interrogating her about where she's been when he hasn't been able to reach her. — Louise, mother of Vanessa, 14

Ask your teen why she is so jumpy, nervous or afraid to displease or disagree with her boyfriend. Does she flinch when he lifts his hand to do something? In an outburst of anger does he hit a wall or break something? Have you heard stories in which your daughter was not threatened directly, but was frightened by his temper or his violence towards someone or something else? These and other signs of fear are important warning signs.

Does her boyfriend check up on her?

> We spent all of our time together . . . but it became obsessive: I was either with him or talking to him on the phone. At one point, I even had to be on the phone with him when I went to sleep so that he knew I was at home at night. I was allowed to talk to only two people at school—both were girls, and he had his friends watch me to make sure I was obedient.
>
> — Salina, 13

You may see evidence that your daughter is being watched, followed, checked up on. You may see her boyfriend happening to show up everywhere you go. The most common sign is the constant phone calls. The calls are often tension-filled and contain repeated explanations and apologies from your daughter, as if she were being interrogated about everything she wears, does, and says and with whom. You might find out that your daughter's boyfriend is calling her sister, brother or friends to find out where she is or what she is doing, or to check up on her behavior, dress, contacts with friends and so forth.

Vicki describes her experience with her fifteen-year-old daughter Jenny:

> One night we decided on the spur of the moment to walk up the block for an ice cream cone. Outside our door, I noticed movement behind parked cars. Greg [her husband] investigated and discovered Jenny's boyfriend Mark and his friend crouching behind the cars, watching our house. Another night, at midnight, I heard noises at Jenny's second-floor window. She and I looked out to see Mark standing below.

Does he verbally lash out at her, call her names or talk mean to her or about her?

If he does these things, he is emotionally abusive. People

often do not recognize this kind of behavior as abusive. Verbal attacks can be especially damaging because they undermine a person's self-esteem. As a parent, it is important for you to know that often the extent of the abuse is actually worse than what you have witnessed.

Does your daughter seem to be giving up things that were important to her, such as school, friends, time with family, activities, interests?

You may notice that your daughter is not doing things she used to enjoy, or is not doing as well in school as she used to. She may be spending so much time with her boyfriend, and be so consumed by the relationship, that she stops paying attention to anything else. When she tries to see her friends, he gets angry, accuses her of cheating on him or convinces her that they don't need other friends or time apart.

You may find out that your daughter is having difficulty concentrating in school. Your daughter's comments or explanations may alert you: "Ricky says that only really nerdy kids play soccer, and besides, he wants me to spend all of my time with him. Isn't that great?" Or: "Andrew thinks all my friends are dumb and spoiled. I don't know. Maybe he's right."

Parents may be unhappy about these kinds of changes in behavior even without suspecting abuse. But they are signs of emotional abuse, even if not necessarily physical abuse.

Does she apologize for him and his behavior to you and others?

You might notice your daughter apologizing and making excuses when her boyfriend does things to upset her. She may not acknowledge that she feels bad when he hurts her. Instead, she blames herself for his mistreatment and defends him, justifying why he has treated her badly. She is protective of him, seeing him as misunderstood or victimized by others.

Have you seen him be verbally abusive or physically violent towards other people or things?

A clear sign that your daughter's boyfriend is or could be violent toward her is seeing his explosive temper or violence towards other people or things. If you witness or hear that he throws things, or hits walls or people when angry, these are clear indications that he does not control his temper. This kind of explosiveness is intimidating, and just as frightening as violence directly aimed at your daughter.

Has her appearance or behavior changed?

You may have noticed that your daughter no longer dresses well or takes care of her appearance. Something is wrong when a daughter who usually spends time each morning fixing her hair and makeup, and carefully selecting outfits to wear to school, is suddenly having a hard time getting up in the morning and doesn't care about how she looks. She may be covering bruises with long sleeves and turtlenecks, even in summer. Her boyfriend's emotional abuse and jealousy may be making her afraid of other guys' attention. His accusations about how she "comes on" to other guys, and her fear of his violence, may lead her to wear clothes that cover or hide her body. His constant criticisms or erratic violent explosions, along with her isolation, may affect her self-esteem so badly that she is depressed and therefore is not taking care of herself. Neglected appearance is also a major warning sign of sexual abuse or rape.

If your daughter is depressed, she may have suddenly gained or lost a lot of weight. Other signs of depression are sleeping too much or too little, inability to concentrate, withdrawing, not caring about anything, showing little pleasure or enjoyment, and expressing thoughts of suicide.

Sometimes behavioral change is caused by substance abuse. Your daughter may be drinking alcohol or using drugs—as a way to cope, as part of the relationship (i.e., they drink or use drugs together), at his insistence, or indicating a problem she had before the relationship that has now become worse. Some parents have found out about dating violence through dealing with their daughter's substance abuse.

Speaking the Unspeakable: Talking to Your Teen About Sexual Violence

Sexual violence is the most difficult aspect of abusive relationships for teens to talk about. Forced or coerced sex is often part of the cycle of violence along with emotional and physical abuse. Many teens have told us that the abuse in their relationships started with forced sex.

Your daughter may not have defined her experience as rape at the time that it was happening. She may not be able to acknowledge it fully to herself. If she is sexually inexperienced or if this is her first sexual experience, she may be completely confused about what has happened to her.

She may feel terrible about sex: feeling used, dreading sex, experiencing it as painful. But she may not realize that her boyfriend is using sexual violence to maintain power and control over her. He may not accept it when she does not want sex. He may choose to believe that when she says no she really means that she wants to be talked into it or that she is playing "hard to get." A teenage boy may think that if a girl previously engaged in sexual activity with him, he can automatically expect her to respond to any of his demands for sex. Your daughter and her boyfriend may believe that because they are in a relationship, it is her responsibility to do whatever he wants her to do sexually.

Why Teens Don't Talk About Sexual Assault

Even under "normal" conditions, teens are uncomfortable talking to their parents about anything sexual. In one study, only one in five teens told their parents about being sexually assaulted. Many teenage girls fear their parents' disapproval of behavior that may be associated with the rape—for example, dating without permission, being sexually active, continuing to see a boy their parents dislike, or drinking alcohol or taking drugs. They expect parents not to believe them. They are also afraid that their parents will blame them for the assault rather than offering the support and understanding they need. In some cases they are right.

Teens also may not tell parents about sexual assault because they want to protect them and feel that they can handle the situation on their own. Some teens feel their independence will be compromised if they involve their parents. And some feel their parents don't understand very much about their lives. In addition, many teens don't look at sexual assault as "real rape" because it wasn't committed by a stranger.

Attitudes About Sexual Assault

When we asked high school students to define "acquaintance rape," we got these responses:

- That's not rape; rape is when a guy you don't know grabs you and threatens you with a knife or gun.
- She's his girlfriend; a guy can't rape his girlfriend.
- She wasn't a virgin, so it doesn't matter.
- She kissed him, so it's her fault.
- He took her out and spent a lot of money on her. What did she expect?

Many adults have these same ideas about rape. The truth about sexual assault by intimate partners and acquaintances is quite different. Rape is not committed only by "strangers." Agreeing to kiss or "mess around" does not mean that a woman has agreed to have sex. Everyone has a right to say no to sexual activity and have those wishes respected. If a woman allows a date or her boyfriend to buy her dinner or treat her to a movie, she does not owe sex in exchange.

While you, as a parent, learn about date rape, it is important to maintain a dialogue with your teen to develop their awareness of these realities. Open discussion of sex and sexual violence helps them to recognize date rape, to say no to unwanted sex, and to challenge the pervasive attitudes of their peers.

Effects of Sexual Assault

If your daughter has been sexually assaulted by her boyfriend, you should be aware of the kinds of emotional reactions that often occur. She may experience feelings of guilt and shame. These feelings can be especially strong if she has continued contact with her boyfriend. She may blame herself for not being able to foresee or stop the assault, or for making the wrong choices. She may feel she did something to cause the assault. Other people could be contributing to her feelings of guilt. They may try to find a "reason" for the sexual assault in the same way they try to find a "reason" for battering: by finding fault with her behavior, attitude or dress. Blaming the victim is a coping mechanism that keeps people from feeling vulnerable. "If I find something wrong with her behavior, and I don't do the same thing, then it won't happen to me," they think. Parents may blame feel so angry and powerless when they learn that their daughter has been sexually assaulted that they blame her and direct their anger at her.

It is natural for victims of sexual assault to feel frightened and powerless. Isabel describes how she felt:

I didn't tell anyone about the rapes. After he hit me he would want to make up. He'd feel sorry. Then he would want to have sex, but I wouldn't want to right then. I'd be upset and black and blue. But then he would beg me and get mad and frustrated. He'd throw me on the bed and have sex with me. It felt bad, and I'd imagine myself on the ceiling looking down, like I wasn't really there.

I thought there was something wrong with me. After all, he loved me so much, and he was sorry. He needed sex all the time, and I thought I was frigid or cold. It never felt good to me. Maybe this is just the way sex is.

I hadn't admitted it was rape even to myself until we had been broken up for about six months. I started having nightmares and reliving the rapes. My concentration was gone and I started being nervous around people, especially guys. I'd freak when this guy I just started dating tried to put his arm around me. I was scared to be out with people because I thought they were looking at me, and I sort of felt ashamed of how I looked. I had trouble making the simplest decisions. I lost all confidence in myself. I felt like I was going crazy.

Isabel's reactions are part of a complex set of emotional, physical and behavioral responses known as Rape Trauma Syndrome. The powerlessness and loss of control that rape victims experience are similar to those experienced by victims of other traumas, such as car accidents, earthquakes and hijackings.

Although it is difficult to separate the effects of sexual assault from the effects of being isolated, controlled and battered in a violent relationship, sexual assault has distinct effects on the survivor's feelings about herself and her body.

Young women have told us they have stopped caring about their appearance in order to look less attractive to their boyfriend or to other guys. Others have gained a lot of weight as a "protection" against sexual feelings. Others have had physical problems, such as migraine headaches or stomach pain.

Other symptoms of Rape Trauma Syndrome are loss of concentration, sleeplessness, nightmares, flashbacks, memory gaps, fear reactions of being touched in ways associated with the sexual assault, or of being touched sexually at all, and fear of places or things associated with the sexual assault. Some teens have suicidal thoughts and some actually attempt suicide.

Identifying the symptoms of the syndrome with your daughter will help her realize that she is not going crazy. These are normal reactions to a traumatic experience, and they go away with time and with opportunities to talk about the experience.

What Parents Can Do

By becoming informed, you can help your daughter define rape and sexual assault, identify whether or not she has had these experiences and deal with them.

Ask your daughter in a supportive, non-judgmental, non-blaming way about what is happening in her sexual relationship. Ask her whether she has felt forced or coerced to have sex, or if she has felt afraid to say no to sex. You may both be shy or uncomfortable talking about this. But the effort to overcome the secrecy will allow room to gradually overcome the shame. You will help your daughter think about what has happened to her in new ways. It will be good for her to hear that her reactions are normal, and that she doesn't deserve to be treated this way.

If you feel that you cannot talk with your daughter about sexual abuse, help her find someone she can talk with. If you do talk with her, you will probably become upset when you learn about her experiences. You must consider your own need for support to deal with your feelings. You will need to talk about your concerns, fears and feelings; but your daughter will be unable to listen to your feelings or support you. You might both need to see a counselor. With both of you getting the support you need, you can help your daughter to heal from the sexual violence and be open to positive experiences in the future.

3

UNDERSTANDING THE DYNAMICS OF AN ABUSIVE RELATIONSHIP

We are often asked why teens "allow" themselves to be abused. We are not asked as often why batterers use violence. There is far more focus on why a victim "participates" or "brings on" the violence. Naturally, parents search for a way to understand why a teen would love and stay with a person who is violent towards them.

Most battering relationships are not solely violent, but have tender moments as well. What keeps any couple loving and needing one another is complicated in any relationship; the dynamics of a battering relationship are especially complex. Intermittent kindness and abuse trap the victim in the cycle of violence. We will discuss these issues in this chapter.

But understanding why someone stays with a person who is violent does not explain why the violence takes place. All it takes for a relationship to become abusive is for someone to use violence once. Once batterers act on their violent impulses, they find it easier to use violence again and again. The first part of this chapter analyzes the factors that contribute to a batterer's use of violence.

Why He Batters

It is hard to explain why a person is cruel or violent to someone they love. There is no single explanation for it; a variety of factors contribute to violence in relationships. You may recognize some of the following in your teen's battering relationship. Again, please remember that we refer to the batterer as "he" because it is most commonly, although not always, the case that relationship violence is perpetrated by males.

Jealousy

Many high school and college students say that jealousy is the major cause of dating violence. Although it is based on insecurity, teens often think jealousy is a sign of love. The abuser says, "I love you so much I can't stand for you to have other friends. I want you all to myself."

A girlfriend or boyfriend feels flattered by this proof of love. But they may ignore the way jealousy leads an abuser to restricting and controlling behavior. What starts out as romance and "special" love can become a prison for the person who is loved. Love has already become a prison when an abusive boyfriend says to his girlfriend, "I want you all to myself," and then has jealous, angry explosions when his girlfriend sees her friends or does something she wants to do for herself.

Then, because she is afraid, the abuser's girlfriend tries to avoid the abuser's bad temper and violence. So, gradually she stops doing things or seeing people that are important to her. She becomes more isolated, and more dependent on the abuser as the only person in her life. And the abuser becomes *more* jealous and violent, *not* less. That is because he discovers that his jealousy gives him an excuse to control the person he loves, by keeping her intimidated, frightened and dependent on him.

In fact, jealousy is *not* a sign of love. People are jealous because they are insecure about themselves, and they are afraid they won't be loved. Because they are insecure, they may use their jealousy to dominate and control the person they love.

Asserting Power

In our society, teenagers can learn mistaken ideas about what is normal in a relationship from what they see in movies, on television and in advertising. They see many situations in which a strong person or group maintains power by using violence to control people who are less powerful. They see bigger or older kids bullying smaller or younger kids. They see governments using armies or bombs when they have a conflict. They see women treated badly in the movies or on TV. Then they see that many people think violence is not serious. They may see adults they know using violence to show they have power. So they assume that maintaining power with violence is normal.

Peer Pressure and Gender Roles

Some young men believe it is their right to abuse women. They mistakenly believe that men should dominate and control women, and that women are passive, inferior and obligated to please men.

There is a lot of peer pressure on young men to be sexually active, and sometimes sexually aggressive, with girls. They feel it is their role to be dominant and to control their girlfriends' activities and behavior.

Young men receive approval from their friends for being

"the boss," for keeping their girlfriend "in line" by pushing her around, or for ignoring her when she says no to sex. They may be afraid they won't look "man enough" if they don't behave this way.

Girls often feel pressured to do what their boyfriends want them to do, even if it hurts them. They often become dependent on their boyfriends. They learn to put boyfriends first, and to not have anything important in their lives apart from a relationship with a boyfriend. They are judgmental and critical of girls who are not seeing one special guy. A girl feels peer pressure to be in a relationship even if it is not good for her.

Girls feel pressured to have sex when they don't want to. A girl may blame herself if her boyfriend makes her have sex in spite of her saying no. The pressure comes from mistaken ideas about sex and relationships. For example, teenagers often believe that if a guy takes a girl out, she is "obligated" to have sex with him, even if she doesn't want to. Many teenagers believe that guys are justified in raping a girl if they are turned on by her or if they have spent money on her. Once a girl agrees to have sex with her boyfriend, she may believe that she doesn't have the right to say no, or to change her mind or not want to do particular sex acts, or she may believe she doesn't have the right to say no on another date—as if he "owns" her. Or she may be afraid that she will lose her "reputation," and be seen as a "slut" by other teens if she doesn't agree to his "ownership" of her.

Abuse During Childhood

Young men who were abused as children or who saw their mothers being abused are more likely to abuse their girlfriends, wives or children. Studies show that most people who are in prison for committing violent crimes were abused as children. This does not mean that everyone who has been abused becomes abusive. But a combination of factors that includes a childhood history of witnessing or experiencing physical abuse seems to lead batterers to use violence.

A young man may have learned from his abusive parent to blame others for his problems, and to use violence to maintain control. Situations in which he feels frustrated or powerless trigger overwhelming rage. He may have learned to release his tension by exploding and losing his temper, no matter who gets hurt. Feeling victimized, he feels justified when he lashes out at those closest to him, and those with whom he feels most vulnerable. He may not have learned other ways to handle his problems and feelings.

If he has witnessed his mother being abused by his father, stepfather or her boyfriend, a young man accepts the mistreatment of women as normal. In such an environment, he does not learn to treat women with respect.

Insecurity and Anger

Teens who are violent with their girlfriends or boyfriends have trouble handling their insecurities and fears. Different psychological dynamics underlie each individual's use of violence, usually caused by traumatic or disruptive childhood experiences. Three of the more common psychological factors are unmet dependency needs, the fear of abandonment or loss, and the compulsive need to have order and control stemming from a fear of chaos. Although many other people have these fears and insecurities and do not become violent, batterers may be affected by these and other factors that influence them to use violence rather than other means of coping.

Dependency needs are stimulated when a batterer falls in love. He finds himself to be emotionally needy and dependent on his girlfriend. When these needs are stimulated, and he then perceives them as not being met, he becomes panicky and enraged. He may also feel that it is unacceptable and unmanly to be dependent, so he restricts and undermines his girlfriend until she becomes dependent on him, and then he can hide his own dependency.

Batterers who experience an intense fear of abandonment become panicky and enraged at the perceived threat of loss, especially of being left. They are afraid their girlfriends will leave them, so they have trouble trusting them. They constantly test their girlfriends to prove their love, including the demand that they give up everything to be with them. At any real or imagined sign that their girlfriend might think of leaving them, they become violent.

Batterers who need order and control fear that everything around them will fall apart if they are not in control. They demand that their girlfriends comply with their compulsive requirements for attention—for example, with frequent and poorly timed demands that she bring him things instantly, meet him at particular places or rescue him from his daily troubles and inconveniences. Batterers become enraged, and violent, when they do not get their way.

Batterers don't know how to communicate or to talk about their feelings. They don't empathize or understand how their girlfriends or boyfriends feel afraid and upset when they get angry and treat them badly.

Alcohol and Drugs

Many teenagers who have experienced violence say that drinking alcohol and using drugs make it worse. Alcohol and drugs allow a person to lose her or his inhibitions and become violent. Research has not proven that there is any direct causal relationship between substance abuse and violence. However, they have often been described as exacerbating one another, like pouring gasoline on a fire.

People do change when using alcohol and drugs. Their perceptions, reality and reactions are altered. Some drugs trigger violent behavior. Some people are able to control their violence when they don't drink. For others it doesn't make a difference; they are violent whether or not they are drinking.

A guy gets drunk at a party, takes his girlfriend home, and verbally and physically attacks her. Later he explains that he gets violent when he drinks. However, at the party, he was able to decide *not* to beat up other people. He saved his violence for his girlfriend. If he had decided not to drink, he might have been able to decide not to beat up his girlfriend, too. So he uses his drinking as an excuse to be violent towards his girlfriend. Abusing alcohol and drugs is often a dangerous way of avoiding personal problems. Problems with substance abuse and problems with violence must each be dealt with separately.

As complicated as all the contributing factors can be, for a batterer to stop using violence he must realize that only he can stop it. He is responsible for his violence and for making the commitment to change his behavior.

Why She Stays

The question that parents of abused girls most often ask is "Why does my daughter put up with the way her boyfriend treats her?" Your daughter may be furious with him for hurting her, and the next day she may be in love again, or she may make excuses for him as if she had never been angry.

You may see her go back and forth as she changes her mind over and over again.

You may be wondering if there is something wrong with your daughter, or with the way you brought her up. You may be continually trying to figure out why she goes back to her boyfriend after she has been hurt by him. The same questions arise if it is your son who is being abused, but then you may also have concerns if you believe your son is not "acting like a man."

Ultimately, most teens do leave battering relationships. It may take weeks, months or years, and they may break up and go back several times before the relationship finally ends. In the meantime, there are a variety of reasons why girls keep seeing their boyfriends in spite of violence. In this section, we will discuss what girls have told us about why they stay, and how a phenomenon called the "Hostage Syndrome" affects the way girls perceive what is happening to them.

Hope, Fear and Love

Girls have told us that hope, fear and love keep them tied to the young men that hurt them. Most of the girls we have talked with who have ended a battering relationship had tried to break up several times before finally doing so.

> I'd try to break up with him, then he'd cry and say, "I'm sorry, don't leave me. I'll stop hitting you." I'd believe him, because I didn't want to leave him; I wanted him to change.
> — Adaliz, 19

Your daughter may hope that he'll change, or hope that her love will change him, or hope that something will stop whatever problems she blames for his violence (such as drinking, school pressure or conflicts with his parents). She may hope that they can recapture the romance of the beginning of their relationship, or that the good times will last "this time" and not be interrupted by violence.

> Bobbie was always trying to save Josh. "He doesn't have a family," she'd say. Or, "He never had Christmas." Or, "He never had books." She believed that if only she could do enough for him, or give him all the things *she* had, he'd change—because he'd love her so much, he'd become more like her. — Terrie, mother of Bobbie, 16

Fear also keeps girls from breaking off battering relationships. They often discover early in the relationship that the violence intensifies anytime their boyfriends suspect or imagine that they are thinking of separating. Your daughter may be afraid that when she tells her boyfriend she wants to end their relationship, he will explode and be more violent than ever.

Renee said, "Suzanne was afraid to leave him because he threatened to kill her or other guys she might go out with." She may be afraid that he will hurt you or other family members. She may be afraid that he will stalk her, follow her, harass her, threaten her and her friends and family, especially if he has already done these things before.

> She was afraid for us. Josh threatened to hurt the baby (her younger brother), or to do something violent to all of us. So she stayed away from us [with him] to keep him away from her family. — Terrie, mother of Bobbie, 16

Your daughter may have tried to break off the relationship, but her boyfriend became so depressed he deliberately hurt himself, or threatened to kill himself. So she is afraid to try again. She may feel that she is the only one who loves and understands him, and that he needs her so much, he won't be able to survive without her. She may feel more responsibility than love for him, and too afraid of what will happen to him to try to break up.

Other fears also make it difficult to break up. Your daughter may be afraid to be alone, fearing the pain of loneliness without the intensity of this relationship. She may be afraid that she will never again find someone to love her (especially if her boyfriend has been telling her this).

I felt lucky to have him, and believed that no one else would want to be with me; I was convinced that I was ugly, stupid.
— Jessica, 16

Love and expectations about a loving relationship may keep your daughter with her batterer. She may believe that the abuse is normal, that all relationships are like this. Or that her boyfriend's hitting her means that he loves her, and his jealous tantrums show how much he cares. She may expect that once she has had sex with someone, that means they have a commitment to each other, and should get married. If she is pregnant or has had a child with her boyfriend, she may believe that she must always be with him.

Her expectations about her future may affect the way she feels about staying in the abusive relationship. If this relationship is all that she has planned for her future, and she does not see other options, she may be unwilling to give it up. She may believe there are no other guys she would prefer to be with, or that she doesn't have anything else to look forward to, such as work, school, athletics, or other activities.

Love can make it difficult to end a battering relationship. Often the bond between the partners is intense. When the cycle of violence is in the honeymoon stage, and temporarily free of violence, the victim and the abuser may feel strong love or an intense bond for one another.

> [After breaking up and going back:] He was security. I knew that he would be there, that he still loved me. . . . I thought, "Thank goodness I have him again; I need him.". . . . I didn't think I could live on my own, or do anything without Larry. . . . We had such an incredible bond to each other, it was hard to break away. — Deborah, 16

The "Hostage Syndrome"

Research has shown that a phenomenon called the "Hostage Syndrome," also known as "traumatic bonding," adds to the intensity of the bond between abuser and victim.[1] As a result of being traumatized (i.e., having her physical or psychological survival threatened), the victim needs nurturing and protection. If she is isolated from others, the victim turns to her abuser. If the abuser is loving or kind, she becomes hopeful, and denies her rage at him for terrifying her previously. So the victim bonds to the loving and kind side of the abuser and works to keep him happy, becoming sensitive to his moods and needs (hoping he will not hurt her). She tries to think and feel as he thinks and feels, and unconsciously takes on his world view. She sees her parents and others the way her abuser does—as hostile to their relationship, as her enemy, trying to come between them and their great love. Her own feelings, needs and perspectives, especially her feelings of anger or terror, get in the way of her doing what she must to survive, so she gradually loses her sense of self. Even when she has the opportunity to leave the abuser, she has an extremely difficult time doing so. She is afraid of losing what she sees as the only positive relationship she has, and of losing her identity as his girlfriend—the only way she knows herself. She goes back and forth, pushed and pulled between her fear of and her anger toward her abuser and her survival-based desire to take care of and protect him.

Addictive Relationships

Almost all relationships start with romantic love. In romantic love, everything seems perfect, as if this is *the one* person who is right. The couple only sees the good things about each other. Things that one instinctively doesn't like are excused, or seen as positive. For example, what one finds to be "devoted" and "attentive" at the peak of romance may later be perceived as "suffocating" and "controlling."

Romantic love is thrilling, exciting, passionate. As the relationship develops, it can become either nurturing or addictive.

Feeling intensely romantic at first, a young couple wants to be together all of the time. In an addictive relationship, they gradually feel more desperate to be together. They find themselves not doing things that are good for them, just so they can be together. They feel threatened by anything one of them does apart from the other. If one is addicted and the other is not, then one is desperate, jealous, threatened by the other's activities or friends that do not include him or her.

To you, as a parent of a teen in an addictive relationship, your child seems obsessed. You can't get his or her attention to focus on anything except the relationship. Either this relationship becomes part of your family life, or you hardly see your child at all. Your teen is on the phone or waiting for a call whenever he or she is not with the object of their affection.

An addictive relationship may or may not turn into an abusive one. It usually goes on for a prolonged period of time because both partners find it difficult to extricate themselves from each other. If your child is the target of addictive love, he or she has a terrible time convincing the other that they spend time separately, and suggestions of breaking up provoke a huge, dramatic crisis. If your child is addicted to the relationship, he or she experiences what could be a life-threatening panic at the threat or the thought of losing their partner ("life-threatening" because of the threats of violence or suicide that are often involved).

A nurturing relationship, on the other hand, doesn't rely on dependency to sustain the couple. The people involved encourage one another to have friends and to enjoy activities they do separately as well as those they do together. They support each other to do well in school, work and other activities. If they have an argument, neither is afraid of the other. If one wants time alone, the other can accept it. Although they love each other, they know they can survive the painful feelings after a breakup and go on to other relationships if this one ends.

Alcohol and Drugs

Sometimes addiction to crack, cocaine, heroin or alcohol plays a major role in keeping a young woman in a battering relationship. Teens whose partners are addicted to drugs or alcohol are at high risk of violence from their partners. It is well documented that male partners play a key role in initiating young women to drugs and alcohol. Substance abuse is another reason that girls continue to see a boyfriend who is violent. Sometimes the boyfriend is her source of drugs and it is this addiction that keeps her seeing him. She may choose to return to the familiarity and security of doing drugs with her boyfriend rather than searching out the drugs on the street.

Sometimes they drink or use drugs together to sustain the connection between them or her caretaking role. For example, some girls have told us that they drink or use drugs in efforts to make their partners drink or use less; others have told us they drink or use drugs when forced or coerced by their partners; and others have told us that the powerful bond between them and their abusers includes using drugs and drinking together.

Ultimately it is important to understand that victims do leave battering relationships, even if they go back more than once before the final break. A girl's tie or bond to the batterer is only part of the picture in understanding why she stays. Leaving or breaking up can be frightening, dangerous and complicated because of the likelihood that the batterer's violence will escalate when she tries to leave.

HOW A VIOLENT DATING RELATIONSHIP AFFECTS YOUR FAMILY

A battering relationship causes an emotional rollercoaster for every member of the family. Margaret's nineteen-year-old daughter Molly has been seeing William for two years. Margaret says:

> We're walking on eggshells. I'm afraid to tell my husband about her new bruises. I worry about her brothers getting in trouble because they want to beat him up. Molly tells her sister things, and makes her swear not to tell me. Then when she gets hurt, her sister feels guilty and I get mad at her for not telling me sooner. When Molly and William are getting along, she invites him over and she wants us to act as if everything is OK. We've called the police, we've been to the hospital. She breaks up with him. We go through so much, and then she goes back.

If your daughter is in a battering relationship, she probably goes back and forth. She feels close to her batterer when he is not being abusive, and she is secretive or angry with you. Then, after he has been violent, she feels hurt and angry, and may seek support from you. Then they make up and she gets close to him again. As her relationship with him goes back and forth, so does her relationship with you.

It is emotionally wrenching for parents to see a child going through this. The usual teenage emotional rollercoaster of drama and moodiness is difficult enough, but dealing with a battering relationship as well is a nightmare for parents.

Your reactions to her and her boyfriend engage you in their emotional rollercoaster. Everyone in the family—other children or extended family who are close—reacts differently, so you not only react to your daughter and her boyfriend but to one another. The entire family is eventually on the rollercoaster.

Often parents undertake enormous effort and hard work to confront the violence. It is a natural response to try to protect your child. The stress and strain of figuring out what to do, and of dealing with your daughter's unwillingness to cooperate or her resentment of your "interference," can be exhausting. Adaliz describes what her parents went through:

> My parents found out I was still seeing him. My friends would tell their mothers, who would tell my mom. She would question me, but I would lie about seeing him. My father tried to tell me he's bad for me. They did everything they could to stop me from seeing him. . . . [They] hunted for a different school for me. . . . My dad would take me and pick me up [from school] every day. I couldn't go anywhere. I couldn't make calls. My parents answered the phone, and wouldn't let me talk to Richard if he called. . . . All I wanted was to be with Richard. So I ran away from home to be with him. . . . I thought my dad was a mean person. Now I realize that he didn't . . . want me to be hurt. I realize what my parents went through.
>
> — Adaliz, 19

Effects on Parents

The communication between you and your spouse/partner may be different now that so much focus is on your child's dramatic ups and downs. Conflicts with your spouse about your child's situation may seriously affect your relationship as a couple. Think about how this is affecting you. Do you challenge each other about your alliances, feeling torn between your spouse and your child? Perhaps you want, or demand of each other, a united stand in dealing with your teen, but disagree about which approach to take. You may be upset with the way your spouse deals with your teen, or your spouse may be upset with your way. Do you keep secrets from your spouse, to protect her or him? For example, you may try to keep her/him from being frightened or worried, and hide information about how serious the violence really is. Or you may hide information to keep your spouse from becoming explosive. Do you try to keep your teen from being rejected by the other parent? Many parents find themselves in a mediating role, trying to keep trouble from starting between family members.

> My wife and I are two opposing forces. She talks to Nick, even though he's so cruel to our daughter, Patty. I feel like we should take a stand. I have no patience with them, and my wife and I end up fighting about what to do. On the other hand, while I can't talk to Patty or Nick, my wife knows what's going on. Patty confides in her. I hope my wife and I can make it through this. — Don, father of Patty, 14

You and your spouse may react very differently to your child's abusive relationship, and to each incident or situation that arises. One of you (often the father) may be angry and feel betrayed when your child defies rules to see her abuser.

The other parent (often the mother), afraid to push your child away from the family and towards the abuser, may be more willing to compromise on the rules. One of you may refuse to get involved and the other may be preoccupied with your child's being in danger. One of you may be working hard to help your child after everyone else in the family has washed their hands of the situation.

Many mothers have told us of their fears about their husband's violence towards their daughter's abusive boyfriend—even if their husband had never been violent before. They had never seen them so enraged, explosive and ready to do harm to another person. Fathers have told us they feel defied, pushed to the limit, betrayed, unable to cope with the intensity of their anger. However, sometimes it is the father or stepfather who remains calm as the mother becomes explosive.

What Parents Have Told Us About Their Feelings

- I am vigilant, dreading a call from a hospital or police.
- When I can't deal with it anymore, I catch myself thinking it's not so bad.
- I feel I have lost my daughter. I don't know her any more.
- I feel so angry and manipulated when, after helping her, she goes back.
- I feel guilty. What did we do to her that she puts up with this?
- I've done the best I can. There isn't anything else I can do.
- At times I feel hopeful that she's getting stronger. We all are.
- I feel so relieved when she's safe and acts like her old self again.

- My husband and I can't talk about this any more.
- I'm so stressed I can't sleep, I've lost weight and I'm smoking two packs a day.

There may be more than two parents in your family—for example, if parents have divorced and remarried. There may be more adults involved than just parents—for example, if your child is also being raised by grandparents or other extended family members. Parental relationships may not be easily defined as "married"—for example, if parents are gay men or lesbians, or if a parent is newly involved with someone who participates in the parenting. A more complicated constellation of family members can make it more difficult to deal with the abusive relationship; on the other hand, it can offer more sources of support. A teen may find it easier to seek help from a stepparent, a grandparent or another adult in the family. You, as a parent, may find it easier to get support from an adult who is not the other birth parent of your child. For example, if both birth parents are overwhelmed and blaming themselves and each other, another parenting adult may have a clearer perspective.

Effects on Siblings

Sisters and brothers get less attention as normal family routines are repeatedly disrupted. Depending on how old they are, siblings may not know much about their sister's problems, but they cannot avoid being affected by the repeated crises.

Some children begin to be extraordinarily good as they try to avoid causing trouble the way they see their sister doing. Other children act in ways that will get your attention, as if they are trying to compete with their sister. And others seem to go on with their own lives as if nothing is happening, coping well but covering up their feelings.

If they are older, they may know a great deal about what is going on, and they may get involved, as a confidant(e) of the daughter who is being abused, as witness to the abuse, or as part of their sister's social circle. If they know more than you know, they may feel guilty or conflicted about telling you what they know. They may be trying to help, and feel overwhelmed because they are too young to do anything. They may not understand the seriousness or the complexity of their sister's problems. They may feel angry with their sister and her boyfriend, and not know how to deal with their anger. They might feel protective of her and angry with her at the same time. They might feel confused about how to respond to you and your emotional ups and downs, wanting to be supportive of you at some times and finding themselves angry or upset with you at others.

What Sisters and Brothers Have Told Us

- I'm scared by how upset my parents get with my sister.
- Sometimes I feel as if I've lost my sister. She has changed.
- What do I have to do to get attention around here?
- My dad's right. They should kick her out. I don't get why they put up with her.
- My sister used to be fun, and now all she can think about is her boyfriend.
- She's so moody: happy one minute and miserable the next.
- What's the big deal? He's an OK guy. He's nice to me.
- I can't tell my parents. She'll kill me if I tell.

5

GETTING OFF THE ROLLERCOASTER

Victor has been stepfather to Emilia, fifteen, and Gloria, twelve, since he married their mother Rosa five years ago. Emilia was just starting to date, and Victor and Rosa were worried she was in a situation that she was too young to handle.

I didn't like Thomas from the beginning. Why would a twenty-three-year-old guy be interested in a fifteen-year-old girl? He could only want one thing. Emilia was head over heels crazy for him. Her mother and I tried to give her rules. She had a curfew; no calls after 9:00 P.M.; she could only go out one night a week. She kept defying us. She climbed out the window to be with him. She ran away.

We went to his house and got her and brought her home. Then we decided this was crazy, and we let him pick her up at the house. At least she wouldn't keep sneaking out.

Then one day he picked her up, and I heard yelling outside. I went out, and I saw Thomas yelling at Emilia, trying to push her into the car. She was scared and didn't want to get in the car. I headed for the door, and I saw him grab her arm real hard. I was livid, and I got in his face. "You want to hit somebody? Hit me!" Rosa called the police. That's how we found out. On top of everything else, this guy had been pushing Emilia around and threatening her all this time. He hadn't punched her or anything like that, but he was always scaring her and manipulating her, playing mental games. For the next couple of months, things kept escalating as we tried to keep her away from him. We even thought of sending her to Mexico to live with her grandmother for a while.

Then we realized this wasn't working. We couldn't keep her under lock and key, and this was consuming us. We didn't do anything as a family any more. We were so busy policing Emilia, we were missing Gloria's soccer games all the time. Gloria was upset and moody, and began acting up to get our attention. Rosa and I were always fighting about what to do about Emilia.

So we decided to get off the rollercoaster we were on. We had to slow down and get our minds off this. Rosa and I talked. We realized we had been so busy fighting Emilia, we hadn't even noticed that she had not only pushed us away, but also her friends. Her life was falling apart. We decided that every week we were going to do something as a family, and as a couple. We started to take time out to talk with Emilia and Gloria more. We were determined to have fun again. For the first time in months we went to the movies. Sometimes Emilia would come with us, and sometimes she even enjoyed herself. No matter what, we went to Gloria's soccer games. We even arranged to go away for a weekend.

Victor is convinced that this was a turning point in his and Rosa's ability to understand and protect Emilia and their family from the chaos caused by Emilia's relationship with Thomas. He also believes that after this, Emilia began to notice the effects of her relationship on her family, and tried to slow things down with Thomas. Emilia continued seeing Thomas although he became increasingly violent. She tried to break up with him twice, and a year later, she made the final break.

Taking Quiet, Positive Action

We often overlook the impact of our "quieter" actions. The dramatic intensity of your child's situation can make you feel you are doing nothing when you are not directly confronting the violence or physically moving your child away from the batterer. Or the dramatic intensity may make you feel frozen and passive, unable to think clearly and take any kind of action when necessary. We believe that quiet, positive actions, far from "doing nothing," can have a positive impact. These are times when, alert and aware, you *gather* or *use* or *share* information.

Get off the rollercoaster for a moment whenever you can. When you feel overwhelmed with pain or with fear, take a deep breath, and have a quiet conversation with yourself. Tell yourself, "I am doing the best I can." Tell yourself, "Quiet moments are as important as dramatic actions, and right at this moment, I am doing a great deal."

Quiet moments with your child can allow loving gestures and expressions of appreciation. They can allow you to connect or communicate about aspects of your life together that have nothing to do with violence. They can give you both strength.

The way you manage your reactions and make decisions about your actions will influence the rest of your family, including the teen who is being abused, as you all experience the cycle of violence.

This does not mean that reactions and actions are not helpful. At times, dramatic actions can be effective. At other times, silence is most effective. Your intense reactions can motivate you to be alert, to think creatively and act quickly. It is important to plan, and to take major steps when needed to keep your daughter safe. It is important to be ready to act when necessary, or when your daughter is ready.

Your observations will help you figure out what your child needs from you. Your heightened awareness will help guide your decisions and actions. Quiet comments about your observations help your child know that you see what is happening. Such comments give your child a chance to look at the situation from a different perspective. An empathetic comment that is non-confrontational and does not require a response can have an impact. For example, "Toni, I noticed that when you told John you were going to study with Linda tonight, he accused you of going out with some guy. It must be upsetting when he gets so jealous." This allows Toni (1) to know that you know, (2) to feel that you understand, and (3) to feel upset about John's jealousy if she was about to minimize and deny it. An additional positive statement of encouragement can strengthen Toni's ability to resist John's controlling jealousy: "I'm pleased to see that you are going to study with Linda for that exam tomorrow, even though John might be angry with you. I know how hard it can be to decide to do something that might upset him."

Similarly, an expression of concern based on your observations can go a long way. "Toni, I've noticed that in the last two days John has been mean to you on the phone. I could tell because I could hear you apologizing over and over. I'm worried about how it affects you, how bad you feel about yourself when that happens." This allows Toni (1) to know that you know and care, (2) to not have to do anything to defend herself or John, and (3) to notice for herself that John's mean talk has an effect on her.

Reach out to your other children. Assume they are affected by the disruptions caused by their sister's violent relationship, even if they don't express it. Make sure they understand why you are upset, and help them cope. Talk to them about what's happening, within the limits of what they can understand at their age. Help them with their relationship with their sister and, if appropriate, with her boyfriend. Help siblings do what is possible within the constraints of the situation to actively and directly deal with their relationship with their sister.

Asking and Listening

Asking and listening are quiet, positive actions. Seeking information requires asking questions and listening carefully to the answers you receive. Ask your daughter about what is happening to her, how she perceives it, how she feels about it. If you are not accusing or challenging her, and not requiring yourself to do anything about what she is saying (except to ask questions and listen to her answers), you may learn a great deal.

Passive listening—that is, saying nothing—can demonstrate support and acceptance (of your daughter, not the violence). It is a "potent nonverbal message" that communicates acceptance and fosters constructive growth and change.[1] For example:

Parent: "Toni, you look upset."

Teen: "I am upset. John gets so jealous! He doesn't want me to study with Linda tonight!"

Parent: "Oh?"

Teen: "He can be so mean! He actually thought I would lie to him and go out with somebody else."

Parent:	"I see."
Teen:	"He doesn't trust me. I hate it when he doesn't trust me. He's making such a big thing of this. Maybe I shouldn't go to Linda's."
Parent:	(Silence)
Teen:	"I don't know how to make him trust me."
Parent:	"That's hard."
Teen:	"He has to believe me. I can't deal with this. I'm afraid I'm going to fail my exam tomorrow. I have to study with Linda tonight. She said she'd help me. John will just have to believe me. I want to pass this exam. I'm going over to Linda's."

In this situation, the parent's passive listening—and implicit acceptance and support—enabled Toni to express her feelings, to think about the problem (trust), and to make her own decision.

Ask your daughter's friends and other people who see her with her boyfriend to tell you what is happening. If they are reluctant to tell you, ask them more than once. Let them know that you want to hear from them because you are worried about your daughter, and that they might be able to help her if they confide in you.

They may be relieved that you asked. They may have been afraid to take the initiative to tell you because they thought they would betray your daughter. After ending battering relationships several girls have told us that they were relieved their friends told their parents about the violence, even though at the time it made them mad. The friends didn't know what to do, and felt burdened with the responsibility. People at your daughter's school—teachers, the nurse or counselor, the vice principal—may know about the violence, but assume you also know or for some other reason do not call you. Openly asking about it, finding out whatever you can, and making connections with others make it possible for everyone in your daughter's life to work together to help her.

Gathering Information

Gathering information from all kinds of sources and becoming as informed as possible is also quiet, positive action. You are reading this book, so you are already doing this. Get information from other books, and from videos and television shows. Contact professionals, police officers and others who can tell you what you need to know about options for taking legal action or for getting other kinds of help. Your local domestic violence program or hotline can offer information and help you begin to develop strategies for your particular situation. They may have services that are available to your daughter, to yourself or to the abuser.

Often the information you obtain is not immediately useful but will prove useful at some point later on, and you will be prepared when you need to be.

Joan's daughter, Trudy, recently broke up with her boyfriend because he was possessive and had beaten her up. He was harassing her by showing up at work and threatening her. The first time Joan called the police, they did not intervene because they didn't think there was enough evidence of an assault. Then Joan went to the police again, not to make a report, but to get information about what she could do. She talked to a helpful detective who told her about a prior arrest of her daughter's boyfriend for beating up another girl. She also got information about what the police need to make an arrest. The next time she called to make a report, she was better equipped to get the police to take action.

• • •

Getting Help for Yourself

Getting help for yourself is also important. You cannot go through all of these crises alone. Your child is in danger, you are deeply affected, and you need to talk about it. You are limiting your effectiveness if you keep the abuse a secret.

If both parents are present and involved in the life of the child who is being abused, it will be most helpful if you can support each other. You also need support from family members and friends. You might consider getting help from a counselor or a support group. You may already have thought about counseling for your child. How about counseling for yourself and/or others in your family who are being affected by the violence?

Setting Limits

To get off the rollercoaster, you must set limits regarding the impact on you and your family of the ups and downs of your daughter's relationship.

When you find yourself rushing to rescue your daughter, or punishing her, stop and ask yourself, "What am I doing? Do I want to police my daughter every minute to make sure she does what I want her to do? Do I have to stop everything and respond this minute? Am I being effective?"

You are not being effective when the chaos of your daughter's relationship is controlling you. You don't have to be thrown into a crisis every time she is. You can choose to respond rather than over-react and become over-involved by (1) limiting your own availability to being drawn into the crisis beyond the point that you can be effective, and by (2) setting clear expectations and consequences of your daughter's behavior. Setting limits also makes room for maintaining other relationships in the family.

As Paula said, "There's a limit to how much I will allow my life to be disrupted. There are times when you have to walk away and go on about your life." Paula and Frank were able to have a relationship with Sandy, seeing her every day, living in the same house, without being totally controlled by Sandy's boyfriend Alan and his drug abuse and violence. Sandy knew what she could expect from her parents, and saw Alan away from their house. She knew that she could live in her parents' house, but they would not allow Alan to be part of their lives or to come into their house.

There are several elements in effectively setting limits with your teen. You can let her know what is expected of her and why, and what she can expect from you. The expectations must be realistic and clear, and must focus on specific behavior. The consequences that will follow if she does not meet your expectations must also be clear, logical and natural. Of course, you must be able to follow through with the consequences, provided they fit logically with the expectations. For example:

Parent: "I expect you to be home by midnight or to call by 11:30 from wherever you are."

Teen: "I can't control when we get home. It's up to Bob."

Parent: "You are responsible for getting home on time or calling. Do you mean that you can't come home because Bob won't let you?"

Teen: "Why do you have to make so much trouble? Can't I just go out and have fun? I don't want Bob to get mad."

Parent: "Are you afraid to make Bob mad? Is that why this is upsetting you?"

Teen: "Yes. I wish you didn't have to get so worried."

Parent: "Let's see how we can work this out so that you can be home on time. If we do not hear from you or see you at home by midnight, we *will* worry. We will be awake and assume that you have been hurt. I will call Bob's house, the hospital emergency room and then the police to try to find out if you have been hurt. You have a couple of choices. If you like, I will tell Bob that I take this seriously, and that I expect him to. Or I can pick you up at midnight. Are there any other ways to make it possible for you to be home on time?"

Teen: "If he won't bring me home, can I call you to come pick me up?"

Your tone of voice is crucial. It reflects your attitude, and can make the difference between whether the same words are firm or punishing. It can also make the difference between conveying the message, "That is my limit" or the message, "I dare you to push me past my limit."

Positive interaction between you and your teen will improve her follow-through after you have set limits. When parents are distressed about their children's behavior, they often focus on the problem behavior, and teens often stop paying attention. Abused teens need encouragement and reminders of their strengths. Positive interaction can come from comments from you that are specific to the situation, for example, "You were so clear in that phone call to John!" or "I appreciate that you have been doing the dishes in the middle of this turmoil." This is more effective than general positive comments such as "You are so beautiful."

Setting limits and following through take time to be effective, especially if you are changing your approach toward your teen. They take patience and practice.

Managing Your Anger

Anger is a common, natural feeling, especially in reaction to your child being treated badly. Anger can also be an overpowering emotion. Often parents and siblings, especially fathers and brothers, experience an intensity of anger they have never felt before. It can be frightening, both to yourself and to others who are afraid of what your anger could lead you to do. Dealing with anger can become a problem in itself. When your anger controls you, you can't think or act clearly. You can't be helpful to your family. It can magnify and compound the other problems of dating violence.

The Cabrillo family was so afraid of how Mr. Cabrillo would react that they didn't tell him about the abuse for five years, until his daughter was out of high school. He said,

> It was difficult for me. I didn't find out about it until two years before it ended. My wife needed my support but I couldn't give it to her because I didn't know what was going on. When I did find out, I was furious. I challenged her boyfriend. I wanted to see if he would do the same thing to a man. I started to do the very thing that they were afraid I would do.

When one person in a family is controlled by his or her anger, the whole family can get pulled into an escalating cycle of violence not unlike that of a battering relationship. The family focuses on the potentially violent family member. Many parents have told us that this has been one of the most frightening aspects of the way their teen's battering relationship has affected the family.

This fear became a reality for Julia's family, which was torn apart when her seventeen-year-old brother, Anthony, killed her boyfriend. He became enraged at Ernie for beating up his sister. Anthony was convicted of first-degree murder, considered premeditated because he went looking for Ernie after he saw Julia with bruises and a black eye. He said he intended only to scare Ernie, to get him to leave Julia alone. But he lost control and stabbed him to death.

Dealing with Angry Feelings

Feeling angry is not the same as losing control and becoming verbally or physically violent. It is important to contain and control how you handle your anger while you feel it. You have choices about how you deal with your anger. You also have choices about what you do to contain your anger rather than letting it escalate. For example, if you are angry and more likely to unleash your anger in destructive ways when you have been drinking beer, then it is important to make the choice not to drink beer. Mixing anger with alcohol or drugs is dangerous.

Without outlets for your anger, it builds up. Consider using physical outlets for the tension associated with anger: exercise, physical work (such as yard work), tearing up old newspapers, batting baseballs or hitting tennis balls. Some people find they can release their anger by going somewhere by themselves (even to the bathroom) and yelling. Studying martial arts can provide a good outlet. These outlets don't hurt anyone or anything.

Distractions can help. Focus on something else. Give yourself a break from the situation. Do something to take care of yourself. When you feel your anger building, you can do something to cool off, such as taking time out to calm down before talking about it any more. Some parents find that taking a walk, meditating or praying helps to calm them. It is best to find your own way to relax or calm yourself.

You can use your support systems to help you deal with your anger. Talking and venting with a friend or a family member can help. Family talks about the situation and discussing feelings about it can be constructive. You can use an Alcoholics Anonymous approach by seeking support when you feel you might lose control. For example, you can make an arrangement with a friend (the equivalent of an AA sponsor) who you can call any time you are afraid you are going to explode. The friend can help you talk through what you are feeling and to find alternative ways to handle your anger without hurting yourself or someone else.

Another way for family members to support each other in dealing with anger is to make a plan to ensure that anyone can vent anger safely. Any time a member of the family feels overwhelmingly angry, or when an incident occurs that triggers anger in all of you, you can do the following: give each person four or five minutes to vent their feelings while everyone else listens without commenting other than with noncommittal responses. This means not taking each person's anger personally, but simply listening. This technique can leave everyone free to do problem-solving.

It may seem odd to be reading about how to manage your anger towards someone who is hurting your family because of that person's inability to manage his or her anger. But you have to manage your anger, because the batterer doesn't, and you want to do what you can to keep from escalating the tension in the situation.

De-escalating Anger

We have been discussing managing anger on an ongoing basis over a period of time, which is necessary if a battering relationship is prolonged. But how can you manage your anger in particularly explosive incidents? If you are in an argument with someone, or face to face with someone who is being defiant—your teen, the batterer—what can you do to de-escalate the situation?

There are several ways to approach someone who is argumentative and explosive so that you are not provoked into losing control over your anger. Sitting down is less menacing and defuses the confrontation. Do not respond to baiting or argumentative comments; let the other person vent until they are worn out. To do this effectively, do not disagree or argue, but respond by acknowledging the other person's feelings: for example, "I know that makes you mad" or "That's really terrible." If you disagree with what they are saying, acknowledge that you understand how they feel, and save your feelings for later.

Respond in a quiet voice. Do not attempt to be heard over the other person's yelling by shouting in a loud voice. A softer voice invites the person who is yelling to stop and listen. You might invite the other person to sit down or to take a walk while you talk. Never get in a car with someone who is explosively angry. If the person tries to leave, let him or her go. Don't corner or restrain them. Don't try to touch or enter their physical space, even to try to calm them down. You can only do this when the explosiveness is winding down.

Let them cool off. It is essential that you resist your own urge to explode, or to insult them. If you feel your own anger escalating, take deep breaths, count, come up with an image of a peaceful scene, whatever you can do to keep yourself from losing control. Walking away or leaving can sometimes cool down an explosive situation, but sometimes it can escalate it. Use your judgment.

These techniques apply to an argument or confrontation,

not to a violent situation. Once physical violence starts, you must focus on your own safety and forget about trying to do anything else. If you are a parent of a battered teen, you might help her learn these techniques to help her de-escalate a confrontational situation. She may need to examine ways in which she escalates the explosiveness of a situation rather than taking care of her own safety. It is natural for someone who has been abused to get angry, and because it is dangerous to express it directly, the anger builds. But if her anger gets out of control, she may not make wise choices about how to deal with it safely. This can trigger an escalation of the batterer's anger to the point that she gets hurt. For example, if he is exploding or tense, and she gets "in his face" and escalates the argument, then she is not taking care of herself. If she doesn't allow him to cool off or to leave if he needs to, she may be endangering herself.

This doesn't mean that she provokes violence. She has no control over whether or not he becomes violent, but she can be as careful as possible to not be in his "line of fire." In a battering relationship, it is not safe for the battered teen to express her anger. In a healthy relationship, there is room for arguing and disagreement without fear, control, intimidation, threats and beatings.

Parents can discuss with their teens ways in which they can protect themselves, and how to handle their anger in situations in which they could be hurt because of the threat of danger from violence. This does not stop the cycle of violence, but helps to manage incidents that have the potential for escalating into violence.

Resolving Conflicts Between Parents

You and your spouse or partner may not agree about how to handle day-to-day conflicts with your teen and her boyfriend. Talk to each other. Try to come to some understanding about how each of you feels. Try to accept one another's feelings and limits, validating the struggle each of you is going through.

If you are the spouse of someone who needs help managing their anger, or if you are frightened by the other person's anger, assess the situation. Would or does he or she *act* on their anger in a way that hurts someone or gets them into trouble? If not, allow their feelings to be expressed. If their anger is potentially harmful, set limits regarding your tolerance of their behavior. For example, you can say, "I understand how angry you feel, but you must stop this. You can't blow off steam this way. Everyone's afraid of what you'll do. You're making the situation worse." Of course, this won't work in the middle of their rage when they can't listen. At a quieter time, apply the techniques for managing anger described in this chapter.

6

STRENGTHENING YOUR RELATIONSHIP WITH YOUR TEEN

Tanisha met Tyrone when she was seventeen, in her last year of high school. Tyrone was nineteen and working as a mechanic. Barbara, Tanisha's mother, describes their relationship and the family's way of dealing with it.

> Tyrone seemed like a nice guy. He was certainly devoted to Tanisha. He was calling and coming over all the time. Then one Sunday we were going to church, and Tanisha was wearing sunglasses and a big hat that hid her face. I saw bruises on her ankles, and I asked her what happened. Tanisha said, "Don't worry, we were just in a little car accident last night." She showed me her black eye, and I knew, this girl was not telling the truth. After denying it, she finally admitted that Tyrone drank too much at a party the night before. He beat her up because he thought she was looking at some other guy.
>
> Later, we talked some more, and it turned out that Tyrone drinks a lot. He is also very jealous, and there had been other instances of his getting out of control.
>
> Tanisha is a girl who stands up for herself. She's outspo-

ken. But around Tyrone, she turns to mush. I told her, "You deserve better. What are you going to do about this?" She said, "I won't put up with this. It'll never happen again."

Well, over the next two years, it happened again and again. She moved in with him. She'd still come around because we're a close family. She'd cry to me and ask my advice. I'd say to her, "You need to find the strength to get out." I'd tell her to pray. She knew she could come to me. I understood what she was going through.

I prayed a lot; I was so worried about her. I was glad she also had her grandma to talk to. She's her favorite. We had family meetings. Tanisha's younger brother and sister, her uncle, her grandma and I would talk about what to do. Tanisha was always welcome in our home but Tyrone wasn't. Tanisha wanted us to at least be civil to Tyrone. We all disagreed about what to do. Her uncle refused to speak to either one of them. But I got everyone to realize that Tanisha is making her own choices, and we have to respect that. She's made her bed, and she's going to have to lie in it until she decides she doesn't want to anymore. My mother says, "You can't tell people what to do because they won't listen. Tanisha has to get it out of her system." We, as a family, will never turn our back on her.

After two years, Tanisha realized she was going home to her family more and more often, and finally ended her relationship with Tyrone.

Witnessing your child go through the ups and downs of an abusive relationship often means helplessly watching as she makes foolish, even dangerous choices. It may mean watching the effects of being treated badly for a long time: lack of confidence and self-respect, clinging to scraps of kindness from her boyfriend, sacrificing herself while he thrives. It may mean seeing her angry or feeling powerful one moment, and defeated, beaten down the next.

As your child goes through this, other people tend to withdraw from her the one thing she needs more than anything else: respect. Supporting her self-esteem is especially critical because the battering constantly undermines any positive feelings or beliefs she has held about herself, and worsens any doubts, insecurities or fears she had about herself.

Respecting Your Teen's Choices

You can show respect by listening to your daughter's perspectives. You can indicate that you respect her right to make her own choices, even if you are conflicted and troubled about them. You can ask about her point of view, her feelings and her opinions as well as telling her yours in such a way that you are exchanging and sharing your perspectives without one of you being proven right and the other wrong.

When you are considering ways to deal with the violence, you can include her: "How can we deal with this together?" Your approach can be based on an assumption that she will make the best decisions she can, and build on what she *can* do. You can aim to help her make her own decisions rather than making them for her. Do problem-solving and brainstorming and make safety plans together. Help her understand she doesn't have to go through this alone.

You may not be able to use this approach if she is beyond the point of allowing anyone to talk with her about her relationship. But it is usually possible to find some way to show respect, caring and appreciation of her strengths.

It is important to find all possible ways to build on your daughter's strengths. Notice and appreciate what is working well for her. Encourage her to focus on aspects of and activities in her life besides the relationship, especially areas that have not yet begun to deteriorate, such as school, after-school activities, sports, lessons, hobbies, or friends. You want her to become strong enough to be free of the grip of the battering relationship.

> My fourteen-year-old daughter, Jessica, is a dancer, and when she was seeing Bruce, she began to give up her dancing. I encouraged her to try to continue dancing. I reminded her how much she loves to dance and how strong she feels when she dances. After the relationship ended, she was relieved to resume her dancing without any restrictions imposed by Bruce. — Valerie

You can find ways that your daughter is handling the battering relationship that are healthy or positive. It is empowering to her when you acknowledge how difficult things are for her and that you appreciate that she is trying her best. Recognize and appreciate the ways in which she handles tension, conflict, fear, restricted options. For example:

> *"It must be hard to concentrate on schoolwork, but I am glad you are doing as well as you are."*
> *"I appreciate that you chose to have dinner with your grandparents in spite of the pressure from Jason to see him tonight."*
> *"I know that at times you feel pressure from us to do things with the family at the same time you feel pressure from Jason not to."*

You can strengthen your relationship with your daughter by spending time with her or having conversations that have nothing to do with her battering relationship. It can be a relief to have some time for the kinds of parent-child interactions you used to have before the battering. You might actually have some fun together—watching TV, going to a movie or shopping. Let her know that you value your time together. If you can do this without having a fight about her boyfriend, you will be allowing room for your relationship to be free of his interference.

If your daughter only hears negative comments or criticism from you, your bond with her will weaken, and she will be less able to resist the damage to her self-esteem caused by the battering. When you keep your resentment under control so that it doesn't inhabit every corner of your relationship, you will strengthen your relationship with your daughter. In the long run, supporting her strengths and strengthening the relationship between you can go a long way in helping a victim of battering believe in herself, and to get away from the violence.

Open Communication

What is it about dealing with an abusive relationship that makes open communication so important? Such a relationship often involves patterns of secrecy and isolation that further endanger the abused teen after the abuse has started. The more that your daughter keeps the emotional, sexual and physical abuse secret from family and friends, the more ashamed she becomes. The more ashamed she becomes, the more isolated and the more protective of the relationship she becomes.

If, in addition, he threatens her with more severe violence or death, then she becomes increasingly isolated and terrified. The abuser may also isolate her through jealousy, restrictiveness, excessive criticism and humiliation. This pattern often results in the alienation of the victim from her parents and other people who had been important to her. The more that the abuser succeeds in isolating your daughter from her family and friends, the less protection she has from both the physical violence and the effects of the brainwashing or emotional abuse as they get worse. As isolation increases, violence becomes more frequent and more severe. As a parent, by maintaining your communication and connection with your child, you may be able to interfere with these attempts to isolate her. What is most important is not exactly what you say or don't say, but to keep the paths of communication as open as possible.

Tanisha's boyfriend Tyrone picked a fight with her every time she went to her family's house for Sunday dinner. Barbara said, "We knew that he was trying to get her to stop seeing her family. We kept encouraging her to come. I knew that you have to keep the door open or your child will be lost."

Another reason that maintaining open communication is so important is that the abuse leads to emotionally charged interactions between parents and children. It's easy for communication to be cut off when you and your daughter are both afraid of your temper or of your becoming overwhelmingly upset. Sometimes a situation that could be handled in a straightforward manner becomes a crisis because of a parent's over-reaction. Because such intense feelings and reactions are involved in dealing with violence, extra efforts to initiate and sustain communication are often required of parents. Rosa, eighteen years old, said, "My mom doesn't yell, except sometimes, like when he gave me a black eye, but I'd also be upset if that happened to my daughter. She talks to me, she hears me, she gives me advice. But she talks *to* me, and tells me, "'I know the way you feel.'"

Even under the best of circumstances, teens often keep their feelings or details about their intimate relationships from their parents. Once your daughter knows you disapprove of her boyfriend, she will assume that she cannot tell you anything about him or what is going on between them. She may be afraid of your emotional outbursts about her relationship, or your interference or your restricting her freedom. No matter what you do, there is no guarantee that she will talk to you about her relationship in general, or about the violence in particular. But if you are going to be an effective support for your daughter's safety and for her getting free from the violence, you need to know what she is dealing with, and she needs to know that you can help. *Communication between you is essential for her safety*.

In your day-to-day interactions with your teen, you may find that there are many opportunities to invite her to talk to you about what is going on. You want to talk with her about her feelings and about problems she experiences as well as "information" pertaining to her safety. You don't have to focus on the specifics of her relationship to get a picture of how it is affecting her. According to Thomas Gordon in *Parent Effectiveness Training*:

> One of the most effective and constructive ways of responding to children's feelings is the "door-opener" or "invitation to say more." These door-openers keep your own feelings and thoughts out of the communication process. Young people feel encouraged to open up, pour out their feelings and ideas. [They] also convey acceptance and respect for [her] as a person.[1]

What Gordon refers to as door-openers are noncommittal responses or explicit invitations to say more in response to something your child says: for example, "I see," "Really?"

"Tell me more," "I'd like to hear about it."

Your attitude makes a difference when you invite your child to talk to you. Without a certain attitude, your efforts will be ineffective. For example, you must want to hear what your child has to say. If you don't have time, or if you really don't want to hear about it, it is better to say so, or to arrange to talk at another time. You must avoid inviting her to talk with you, then stopping her with judgments, telling her what to do or over-reacting to what you have heard. You must also be aware when your tone of voice and manner of expressing yourself may contradict your words. For example, there is a difference between asking, "How did you get the bruise on your arm?" with concern (inviting an open response) and asking the same question with anger and blame (triggering a defensive response to your accusation).

You must also want to be helpful, and you must feel empathetic about your child's struggles. You must be able to accept her feelings, even if they are completely different from your own or from what you think she should feel. This is especially hard, and may take time to develop. It also means letting go of your need to control her, and acknowledging that you may help and support her, but that she must actively work on decisions and solutions to the problems she is facing.

There are times when it is important to advise or instruct your teen, or to let her know what you think or how you feel. But the most important tool in communicating with teens is effective listening. And a teen who is listened to is more likely to listen when you express yourself as well.

Effective listening means using open responses that acknowledge your child's feelings, meanings, and perceptions of their problems. Responses allow expression of feelings, understanding and clarification. Responses are non-judgmental and empathetic. They are non-verbal as well as verbal. You notice non-verbal cues ("You look upset"; "You're shrugging and rolling your eyes. You don't agree?"). Effective listening is a first step in problem-solving.

Lucinda has been going with Robert for two years. Even though her parents are distressed about Robert's violence, she says that her friends envy the way she can talk to her parents.

Lucinda: "I have had it with Robert. I told him we're finished, and I don't want him to come around here any more."

Father: "What happened?"

Lucinda: "He's been calling me from jail trying to control everything I do. He gets mad if I'm not home when he calls. He has his friends watching me."

Father: "He has! I thought we didn't have to worry with him in jail! So he's still trying to control you."

Lucinda: "Yes, and I saw a girl on the news who got shot by her boyfriend. I don't want to see Robert any more."

Father: "Oh, my God. Shot! You think Robert could do that to you?!"

Lucinda: "His friends followed me today, and he called and he said, 'I saw you, I was watching you, I know everything you do.'"

Father: "No wonder you're so afraid of him. This frightens me too."

Lucinda: "I never want to see him again."

Mother: "Do you really believe this in your heart?"

Lucinda (in tears): "I really love him. I'm afraid I'll go back to him. But I never stood up to Robert before today. I can't live like this any more."

Mother: "I'm afraid too. How will you get through this, breaking up with Robert, getting away from his friends and

	his threats, but loving him and missing him?"
Lucinda:	"I don't know."
Father:	"It's hard to do what you did today. Maybe you're afraid of what he'll do to get back at you, but you should also be proud of yourself."
Lucinda:	"Maybe I can do this. Do you think I have to move away? What should I do?"

Lucinda's parents listened without jumping in with their own reactions. They clarified what was happening to her, and acknowledged her feelings. They recognized the change in her response to Robert, and supported it. By the end of this conversation, Lucinda and her parents were ready to problem-solve. They all understood that the problem was twofold: how to get away from Robert, and how to deal with the fact that she still loves him and might feel like going back with him.

Are you thinking that this is all fine and well in a book, but this isn't really the way people talk? This example is based on an actual dialogue in a real family. Such a dialogue really is possible for you as well. But no one expects you to suddenly speak as if you are reading from a book. You will find your own way to communicate, and you can use these ideas to add to your effectiveness in a way that is comfortable for you.

Some teens resist advice from parents, and respond better to a problem-solving process in which parents refrain from telling them what to do. How does your child respond when you offer advice? Your child might respond better when it is offered rather than imposed, for example when it is prefaced by, "My way of doing this is. . . . Would this work for you?" or "I have a suggestion. . . . "

It is often helpful to acknowledge the fact that your teen's problems create problems for *you*, too, and for other members of the family. While at times you must set such feelings aside to be able to listen to your child, there are also times that you need to express your own feelings. Your child must know that you are affected as well. How can you express yourself in a way that does not close down communication among members of your family?

Lucinda's parents (above) reacted to what Lucinda was telling them. They expressed their feelings and asked about hers. Some experts have recommended using "I-statements" to let children know that there are consequences to their behavior without blaming, accusing, punishing or using other approaches that make children stop listening or become defensive. An "I-statement" consists of an observation about one's own response to something that someone else is doing, and, if it fits, a request for the other person to change what they are doing. For example:

> *"When I see you with bruises I'm terrified, and I worry about you."*
> *"When I see how Robert hurts you, I get so angry I'm afraid I'll explode."*
> *"When you try to keep it a secret that Robert has been pushing you around, and I can see it happening, I feel so helpless and frustrated. Would you tell me about it? What happened last night?"*

It is often challenging to find ways to give teens information in a way that they can listen to it. Sometimes teens respond when parents share their own experiences. If you have had similar experiences, for example, with a relationship breaking up, or having been battered yourself, telling your teen about it might convey understanding and empathy. It is a way of saying, "I know what you're going through." You can also convey the message that it takes strength to get through these experiences, and that you appreciate her strengths.

You may have a long-term perspective of your teen's experiences that you can share with her. This can be especially true if you have been in an abusive relationship. You can tell your teen, "I've been there, and it was hard. But I've dealt with it. I've gotten out of it." What makes the difference is how you present this. What, specifically, is similar between your experience and your daughter's? Usually the details are not, and teens are interested in hearing about what is most relevant to *them*. Aiming to tell your teen to do as you did is bound to fail. They will tell you it is not the same; and it is important for them to not be the same as you.

You can also encourage your children to communicate with others besides yourself. While you might like them to come directly to you to talk about anything that is bothering them, this is not realistic. They need others to talk to as well. Your teen is safer talking with other adults who are helpful and supportive rather than not talking to anyone at all. It also broadens your teen's safety net if others know what is going on in an abusive relationship and are available to help.

You can be supportive of your teen by acknowledging that she may want to talk to another adult besides you, especially about dating. You can help her to identify someone. For many teens, an older sister or brother, a grandmother, a friend's mother, a school counselor, or a neighbor is approachable and is trusted. They may try out sharing things with someone else, and then find that they are less reluctant to tell you. Your message to your child is still the same as when you encourage them to talk to you: Open communication is important.

• • •

Avoiding Power Struggles

While you are horrified to see your child's batterer controlling her by threatening her, punishing her, restricting her movements and criticizing her, it may come as a surprise to realize you are using these same tactics yourself. You could find yourself in a battle for control over your daughter. Parents who use ultimatums ("It's either him or me!" or "If you continue to see Tim, you'll have to move out!") create or exacerbate a power struggle.

Jennifer said, "My mom told me if I continued to be with him, she didn't want me in the house any more. I was scared of Tim, and I was scared to leave my house, but I ran away to my cousin's house."

Imposing one's power as a means of resolving conflicts is ineffective with teens in general. The outcome is usually that the teen is not motivated to carry out the imposed solution; the teen is resentful of the parent; the parent has difficulty enforcing the solution; and/or the teen has no opportunity to develop self-discipline.[2] Power struggles consume energy and escalate tension, often without resolving the conflict.

Using power and control to resolve conflicts does not work in battering situations in particular. The battered teen feels caught between her parent and her batterer, that she has to choose between them, or that she is controlled by both. Power struggles with parents intensify the difficulty of deciding and acting on what is best (for herself). They undermine her strength and ability to think for herself. They engage her in a fight with her parents rather than collectively struggling with the violence and its effects (on her). Power struggles with a parent align a teen more firmly with the batterer. The bond between them becomes stronger as the parent becomes the enemy they have in common. The battered teen may experience all of these difficulties even if parents do not engage in power struggles about the relationship. Her own struggles with the violence become that much harder for her if parents get caught in battles for control with her.

There are many ways in which parents get hooked into power struggles over battering relationships. A parental ultimatum is similar to what the batterer says and does. He is also telling your daughter that she can't do things she wants to do, "or else." He may be telling her, "It's them or me—your parents want to keep you from being happy, and only I really love you."

Are you trying to control your daughter, for example, by threatening her or threatening to do something to hurt her boyfriend? Are you threatening punishment ("If you insist on seeing him after I told you not to. . . .")?

Are you endlessly arguing, bickering and criticizing her boyfriend, for example, saying: "See, you're failing English again. You know I've told you you'd fail in school if you didn't get rid of James. You don't care about school any more, all you care about is James. Well I hope he'll buy you things you need for the rest of your life because you are ruining your life. . . ."? Do you barrage her with accusations or questions about where she has been, for example, "You think I don't know that you sneak around with that boy. Just where were you until six o'clock? You say you were at the library. Dressed like that? Where are your books? I know what you're up to. Sharon next door saw you two the other day. . . ."?

Batterers do these same things, constantly criticizing what she says, does and wears and how she looks. He may be criticizing her relationship with you, perhaps telling her she is stupid to believe you have her best interests in mind. He may be constantly suspicious and accuse her of lying. Your daughter may be afraid to say anything to her boyfriend because she is afraid to start arguments. She may feel the same about talking with you, especially on the subject of her relationship.

Do you make rules that cannot be enforced? For example, do you say, "You are not allowed to see him ever again," and then find yourself policing her activities: "You aren't going anywhere without me taking you and picking you up."? This also is something that batterers often do.

Do you point out what a loser he is every time he calls or in every conversation with your daughter, the way that the batterer constantly criticizes her family and friends?

How can you avoid power struggles with your battered teen?

Recognizing Your Feelings

It is important to recognize what you are feeling, and how that leads you to act in a controlling manner. Fear, helplessness and anger—at the loss of control over your teen's and your family's well-being—these are feelings that lead most of us to want to control the people or events that are causing them. Acknowledge your fear. Allow yourself to feel that you are terrified that your teen is in serious danger. Accept that you feel frustrated that she "allows herself" to be treated badly. Prepare yourself for the deep sense of powerlessness that comes when you acknowledge that you have no control over your child's choices. This is difficult for any parent. You see your teen in danger and have only very limited ways to protect her. You have no control over the ways in which her choices affect her future or put her in danger. By acknowledging that you have no power in this situation, and by preparing yourself to tolerate these intense feelings, you can begin to let go of your need to control your child. The "Serenity Prayer" can be helpful:

> Grant me the serenity to accept the things I cannot change, the courage to change the things I can, and the wisdom to know the difference.[3]

Using Your Influence as a Parent

Parents cannot control their children, but can *influence* and be a *resource* for them. When you discuss or consult with your children about their behavior, you influence them to make changes themselves. Of course, some parents are able to control their children by making their children afraid of them. Fear of a parent's explosive or violent reactions can make children careful not to do anything that will set the parent off. But this does not lead children to learn to make choices or to change their behavior except to avoid conflict or violence. In fact, it increases their vulnerability to being paralyzed by conflict or violence in other relationships. An attitude of respect for children's right to make choices is most effective in the long run.

It is helpful to distinguish between those conflicts about your teen's behavior that do not tangibly or concretely affect you (even though they might have bothered you) and those that really do affect you, that interfere directly with your life. You can spare yourself a great deal of anguish if you stop trying to get your child to change behavior that doesn't tangibly or concretely affect you. And you will be more effective at setting limits and avoiding power struggles if you focus on behavior that really does affect you.

For example, maybe you are concerned when your daughter spends so much time with her boyfriend that she doesn't keep up with her friends. So you express your concern and offer assistance. But she—and not you—will suffer the consequences and your attempts to get her to see friends will add an unnecessary area of conflict and tension between you. However, when your daughter does not let you know when she will be home after a date, or does not come home at the expected time, it affects you in a tangible way, especially if you are worried about violence. This requires problem-solving with your daughter to come up with a plan regarding her coming home on time or letting you know where she is if she is late.

We are aware that many teens are defiant and refuse to cooperate or to work out solutions to such problems. Sometimes it takes time and repeated efforts on your part to try new approaches that avoid power struggles before your child changes her old ways of reacting to you. Sometimes the influence of the batterer makes her hostile towards you no matter what approach you use. We encourage you to keep trying because at some point the batterer's influence may weaken. Sometimes other factors are affecting your child's behavior, such as alcohol or drugs, or she was defiant, sullen or hostile before the battering relationship.

Liz had been using crack and alcohol, but Peggy didn't know about it. "I thought her wild behavior came from an attitude problem," said Peggy. Attending Alanon meetings or groups for parents of teens can be helpful in situations such as this to help you change ways in which you respond to your child so that you become more empowered.

Developing Effective Techniques for Avoiding Power Struggles

When a conflict seems about to escalate into a power

struggle, you can disengage. This means setting aside your own feelings and listening to and responding to your teen. You do not have to take your teen's actions personally, or interpret her reactions or behavior to be about you. She is not doing anything *to you*. When you disengage you don't get hooked and say things you don't mean. You can sort out your feelings after resolving the conflict with your child, when your feelings won't interfere with your effectiveness.

You can also avoid power struggles and defuse escalating tension by listening calmly and reflectively, and clarifying what your teen feels, thinks or wants. You can ask questions about how she feels or thinks, especially to clear up misunderstandings or miscommunication. You can clarify your perspectives of the conflict. For example:

Teen: "Bob and I are going out tonight. See you later."

Parent: "Where are you and Bob going?"

Teen: "You always have to know everything I do. I can't go anywhere! You're trying to control me. You treat me like a child! Bob's right. He says you just can't face it— your little girl is grown up."

Parent: "You feel that I am treating you like a child when I ask where you are going?"

Teen: "You don't trust me."

Parent: "I think you are very capable and sensible. It doesn't matter how old you are, I think it is safer for someone to know where you are going. That's why I often tell you where I'm going."

Teen: "Well, I don't like all your questions and rules. And I know you don't trust Bob. But everything's OK now."

Parent: "You're right. I don't trust Bob. I know you like him a lot, and that you are happy to be getting along well now. I'm glad to see you happy. But since he hit you,

I've been afraid. I think you still have to be careful when you go out with him. Do you understand how I feel?"

Teen: "I'm not so afraid of him any more. He's changed."

Parent: "Can we work out a way I can feel more reassured by you and you can feel more trusted by me? I will feel more reassured if I know where you are and what time to expect you home."

Teen: "Mom, do you trust me?"

Parent: "Yes, I trust you when I know that you are thinking about your own safety."

What we are saying may seem contradictory. We are saying that it is most effective to respect our children's choices. We are also saying that your child may be in a dangerous situation that affects you tremendously, and you must respond. We are recommending an *attitude* regarding your intervention that reflects your actual lack of control and your respect for your child's rights, and enables effective interventions, not power- or control-motivated interventions.

7

TAKING ACTION TO CONFRONT THE VIOLENCE

Assessing the Situation

It is important to assess your daughter's situation before deciding what is the best course of action for your family. We have found it useful to analyze what information you have or need and the level of risk or danger involved in decisions to take action to protect the battered teen. There are several factors to consider when making decisions about what to do.

Specifics of this batterer and this relationship

What you know about your daughter, her batterer, and the patterns in their relationship enables you to predict or speculate about potential consequences. You can focus on a plan that will work, unique to your situation.

What have you already tried?

What has already been effective? What hasn't? Have circumstances changed, so that an approach that was not helpful before might work now?

Available resources

What resources do you have? Are the Juvenile Division

police officers in your area responsive? Are school administrators or counselors? Do your daughter's friends communicate directly with you and your daughter? Do you have a place your daughter can hide if necessary? Are other resources you need available—funds for travel, other people like friends, family members, etc.?

What else is going on in your family at the present time?

Factors such as your health, the needs of another child or family member, the availability of parents or any number of other circumstances can affect your decisions.

Attitude of the victim

If the victim is ambivalent and has periods of time when she is hurt and angry with her batterer, or periodically breaks up and gets back together, she will respond differently to intervention or planning than will the victim who is more consistently allied with and protective of her batterer. Does your daughter participate in discussions about getting away from the violence, even some of the time? Does she acknowledge your expressions of concern, or does she resist? How likely is it that your daughter will respond to your efforts?

Do you have enough information?

Do you know enough about what is going on in the relationship? Do you know enough about the patterns of the violence? Do you know what resources are available? Do you know what to expect of resources you may use or how to access them?

Risk and Danger

Anticipate the consequences of an action in terms of risk. Will it lead to more violence? What are safety needs that must be considered?

Do you have support from others?

Are friends, family members, school staff, co-workers (yours or your daughter's), a counselor or others aware of your situation? Do they listen and understand? Are there ways in which they can be helpful—to help you cope, to help ensure your daughter's safety?

Planning for Safety

The focus of this section is on a teen's safety, whether she stays in or leaves an abusive relationship. Parents can feel empowered by helping their teen with safety issues. While a battered teen cannot control the violence or the batterer, she is responsible for doing what she can to ensure that she is as safe as possible.

If your daughter is being abused, you can help her to use her strengths to plan for her safety. She knows the batterer and his patterns better than anyone—although she may not realize it until you tell her. She knows what kinds of situations are most explosive for him—and the most dangerous for her. For example, does he become violent when he drinks at parties? What are the safest ways to leave such situations, based on his particular patterns? You can help her remember and take credit for the times she has been strong in dealing with or avoiding the violence.

If she is not going to break up with him, you can try to brainstorm with your daughter so that she is prepared with possible actions she can take when he is explosive or harassing her, or when the tension is building. If she is ready to break up, you can help her make a safety plan to prepare for his explosive reaction to the breakup and the harassment that often follows as he tries to get her to come back.

You can't plan for safety unless you are psychologically

prepared to think of all of the possibilities for which it could be necessary. If you can't face the possibility that your daughter could be hurt, then you can't prepare yourself. This is not the same as thinking constantly of the worst that can happen, and feeling paralyzed by fear.

A self-defense exercise is helpful to prepare yourself. Think the unthinkable: *My daughter could be seriously injured. My daughter could be killed. My daughter could be cut off from me so that we have no relationship. This nightmare is never going to end.* Face your fear. If you feel frozen or paralyzed, think about the worst thing imaginable, and say: *I will deal with this. I will do anything possible to keep this from happening.*

This is a first step toward planning for safety: preparing yourself to take action by making a commitment to deal with the reality of the situation. If you are prepared by being able to think without being frozen by fear, you are better able to handle an emergency situation, and to think about ways to keep an emergency from happening.

There are many different ways to plan for safety. The plans that will work for you depend completely on the particular characteristics of your situation. Brainstorm with everyone in your family, and include others who might be key participants in helping your daughter be safe. Some things to consider:

- Safe places your daughter can go if she can't get home
- Ways to get home safely if violence starts while she is out with her boyfriend
- People she can call in emergencies
- People you can tell to be alert for signs of danger
- Ways to handle specific emergencies, such as: "Go to the hospital emergency room and call me to meet you there"

- Backup for vulnerable times, for example friends to accompany her going to and from school
- Dealing with telephone harassment, for example by using an answering machine
- Steps she can take to be prepared for emergencies, such as spare keys and cash stored where she could get to them (for example, in a magnetic box under her car, or outside his apartment)

Involving Family and Friends

Teen dating violence is everybody's business. However, both you and your teen may not want other people to know about it. Maybe you are embarrassed, or afraid people will think badly of you. You might feel people won't understand why the battering relationship has been going on for such a long time. You might be private about your family's ups and downs in general. Or perhaps you are afraid to involve family and friends in the violence. But you must tell people.

By involving family and friends, you expand your resources for dealing with an extremely difficult and usually dangerous problem. You are creating a safety net and a support system. You are getting the problem out in the open. You are taking it seriously. You are getting strategic support.

Your family and friends are important resources for your battered teen. They include brothers and sisters, grandparents, aunts and uncles, cousins, as well as friends of your family. They can be helpful in many ways. They can provide a place to stay to get away from the abuser. They can be alert for signs of danger and for opportunities to help. They can be supportive and can listen (sometimes more objectively than parents) as your teen makes a decision about breaking up.

They can offer direct opinions without getting the same hostile reactions a parent might get. They can all get together to discuss the situation openly, and provide support and understanding to your daughter, to you, and to one another. They can talk to the batterer so that he knows his girlfriend is not isolated, and he is being watched.

You can join together to plan for your daughter's safety. Your friends and family members also have friends, contacts with other resources, and other ways to expand your network of information and support, and your safety net. Your daughter can feel surrounded by love and support—and by realistic perspectives about her relationship.

Your Daughter's Friends

When you see your daughter's friends, you can ask them about what they see happening in her relationship. If you don't usually see these friends, you can call them or find them at school, at their jobs or in the neighborhood. You can tell them you are worried and why. They may be willing to talk to you if you tell them that while you don't want to get them in trouble with your daughter (if she told them not to tell you), you need their assistance to help her deal with her problems. Teens tend to deny that they are having problems that they can't solve on their own. They tend not to take the initiative to ask parents for help. But they are often relieved when a parent asks for their help because they are afraid or don't know what to do. Good friends of teens who have been badly harmed by their boyfriends have suffered tremendously later when they realized they didn't tell anyone, and then their friend was seriously hurt.

You may be able to give your daughter's friends information about ways they can help your daughter. They can call you if they carry your number with them. They can talk to someone at school who knows about the situation. You can tell them how to contact the police. They can stay close to her and get others to join them when their presence may keep the batterer from hurting her. They can encourage the batterer's friends to talk to him about the seriousness of his problem. You can encourage them by appreciating that they "hang in there" with her to keep her from being isolated.

The Abuser's Family

There are two families involved in a teen's violent relationship: the family of the abuser and the family of the abused. (If you are the parent of a teen who is abusive, also see *Chapter 11*.) If your teen is being abused, you can contact the abuser's family. You may learn more about your daughter's situation. You may find that the abuser's family knows nothing about the kinds of problems their child is having. They may have suspected it, or they may have seen some of the violence themselves, but they may not realize the real scope of the problem. Hearing from you might have an impact on them, and lead them to take the problem more seriously. You may even find that the two families working together can address the problem, and get the abuser the help he or she needs.

Theresa and Joe had talked with Charles' mother about his violence. Charles' mother didn't think she could stop him from doing any of the destructive things he did, especially because of his serious drug problem. But several times she called Theresa and Joe to alert them that Charles was enraged and looking for their daughter, or that he had her there and they should come get her before she got hurt. With these warnings the family was better able to protect her.

Often, the abuser's family is protective and defends their teen. They may not listen, and they may even blame your child. Other families are overwhelmed by their teen's violence, and feel powerless to do anything about it. They may listen, shrug, and say they can't do anything. They may be afraid to see their teen get arrested. Other families may not see their teen very much, or perhaps he lives with a sibling or a friend, and his family doesn't see themselves as being involved in what he does.

There is no way to predict how the abuser's family will react. You may know enough about him to know that his family life is chaotic, or full of violence. You may be right not to expect them to be helpful. But talking with them is a strategy that is often overlooked, and is worth trying if there is even a remote chance that it can help your teen.

In *Chapter 6* you read about how Barbara brought her family together for discussions when Tanisha was not there, so that they could talk about her violent relationship, how it affected all of them, what was going on currently, and how they could handle it. Barbara's family didn't all agree on what to do, but they did agree that they thought and planned better as a group than they did individually. Barbara believes that her family stayed sane through the rollercoaster of Tanisha's two-year relationship because of these discussions.

Neighbors

Your neighbors and (if she is not living with you) your daughter's neighbors can be a part of her safety net. You can tell neighbors what is happening in the relationship, and alert them so they can respond when necessary, for example, to help her directly or to call you if they hear her crying for help. You can also learn about aspects of the abuse from neighbors who have seen incidents outside your house or in your apartment building. For example, neighbors have told parents about an ex-boyfriend stalking their daughter outside their house. Neighbors may be reluctant to "get involved" until you are open about including them. Once you have talked to them, they are more likely to call you or the police, or chase the abuser away, if they see your daughter being harassed or beaten.

Terrie talked to a neighbor in the apartment building where her seventeen-year-old daughter was living with her boyfriend. This elderly woman was afraid of getting involved in the violence she knew was taking place next door. But a short time after talking with Terrie, the neighbor called her when she found her daughter in the front yard, unconscious and bleeding. She saved her daughter's life. That also turned out to be the incident that was the turning point for her daughter, and she began to break away from the relationship as she recovered from her injuries.

Additional Considerations When Breaking Up

Leaving a battering relationship, while safer in the long term, can be extremely dangerous immediately after the breakup. The batterer who feels threatened by the loss of his girlfriend often becomes more violent, or threatens to hurt himself or his ex-girlfriend. When planning to break up, it is essential to prepare for harassment or a potential escalation of violence.

Your daughter's ex-boyfriend may be extremely upset and feel desperately lost after she breaks up with him. He may not believe or accept that the relationship is really over. She may feel torn apart and worried about him. Or, if he is explosively angry with her for leaving, she may be afraid of what he may do to hurt her or her family. She may also find that his anger and desperation lead him to behave in ways that are disruptive, threatening and harassing.

There are several common kinds of harassment after a break-up:

- Constant telephone calls at all hours of day and night
- Having friends repeatedly pressure her during her school day or at her job "not to do this to him"
- Cornering her sisters, brothers, or friends for hours to talk about the break-up and get information about her comings and goings
- Asking her close friends out on dates, or pursuing sexual relations with one of her close friends
- Talking, starting rumors or writing graffiti about her on school property that contains sexually humiliating lies
- Having his friends sexually harass her (name-calling, crudely talking to her, physical harassment)
- Repeatedly waking her up in the middle of the night from outside her bedroom window "to talk"
- Calling or coming to her house and threatening to hurt or kill her or family members
- Forcing her or tricking her into his car or to go somewhere where he barrages her with endless questions and accusations, or pleads and pressures her to change her mind, possibly for hours, while she cannot get away

The ex-boyfriend may begin stalking her. Stalking contains a threat of imminent danger to your daughter and to your family. It can go on for days, weeks, months or years. Most states have recently passed laws against stalking (see *Chapter 8*).

There are a number of common kinds of stalking behavior:

- Making threatening telephone calls at all hours
- Leaving threatening messages on your answering machine, in your mailbox, in your daughter's locker at school, and other places
- Sitting in a parked car or standing outside your home for hours
- Watching her and letting her know in a menacing way that she is being watched
- Following her or having friends follow her
- Showing up wherever she goes, for example at parties or outings with her family and friends

Planning for Safety

In breaking up, your daughter may make a clear separation with no further contact, certain that she no longer wants to be with him. Or breaking up may be a process of telling him she wants to break up and trying to help him deal with it. This process might go on for days or weeks—even months—until she makes a final break and has no more contact with him, or until he accepts that the relationship is over. Another common experience is that when she suggests that they break up, he breaks up with her or goes out with someone else. She then becomes extremely upset and confused about what she wants. She may be devastated that he doesn't want to be with her and become obsessive about being with him.

In general, the major safety concern after the end of a battering relationship is avoiding contact with the batterer, who is volatile. Safety planning usually focuses on her staying away from him, and keeping him away from her.

Teens who have been battered are often hooked back into the relationship because of fear or worry about him: "He needs me."; "He can't live without me."; "It's safer to be with him where I can keep him from hurting my family." They need to get away from his pressure to go back, from his harassment or stalking. They need to get away so they can think clearly. When an ex-girlfriend is around her batterer, she often thinks the way he thinks rather than making her own safety a priority. If he is desperately upset, she focuses on taking care of him, and has a terrible time taking care of herself.

Ending a battering relationship is unlike ending other relationships. It is rarely possible to maintain contact or a friendship after the breakup. It may be possible to work out ways to safely maintain contact if necessary, for example when a child is involved. Often, though not always, it takes extreme measures to avoid contact.

There are many specific techniques for avoiding contact. Here are a few:

- Use a pager or a cellular phone for safety
- Use an answering machine to screen calls
- Save tapes of harassing or threatening calls to use when making a police report
- Change your phone number
- Unplug phones during the night when everyone is at home
- If he has had access to a key to your house, change the lock
- Arrange for her not to be by herself when she is vulnerable, for example if he is likely to confront her on her way somewhere—family members and friends can accompany her for a while
- Alert people at work and school that she doesn't want to

see or talk to him

- Make sure that an adult knows where she is going if it's not part of her usual routine, and when she is expected to return; if you are especially concerned, ask her to call when she arrives at her destination and when she leaves for home
- Remind everyone in the family of emergency procedures, such as how to call 911, with a discussion about the kinds of circumstances in which to follow emergency procedures
- Have her stay with a friend or a family member where he can't find her

Cooperation and coordination between your family and community resources can enhance your daughter's safety. Lisa, a fourteen-year-old, was trying to break up with fifteen-year-old Eric. Several incidents took place at school. Eric pushed Lisa against the wall and choked her in the girl's bathroom, trapping her when she screamed and tried to get away from him. He verbally harassed her, yelled at and threatened her, and called her "bitch" and "whore" across the schoolyard. He didn't believe that she wanted to break up with him, and persisted in following her, writing her love letters and harassing and pleading with her. He had his friends corner her and accuse her of ruining Eric's life.

To try to protect Lisa, a juvenile police officer worked with school administrators. The juvenile police officer and school principal and vice principal let Eric know that they would take disciplinary action according to school protocols if he did not stay away from her. It was clear to Eric that he would be arrested again if he hurt Lisa in any way. Teachers and other school personnel were informed that Eric was not to be alone with Lisa. Lisa and her parents arranged for friends to walk to and from school with her. The domestic violence program in the school educated classmates in general so they were alert and aware, even though they were not told about Lisa's situation in particular. Lisa and her family received counseling through the domestic violence program. Counseling was offered to Eric.

Everyone working out this safety plan agreed that it should not be up to Lisa alone to convey to Eric the seriousness of his problem, or her wish to stay away from him. She was too frightened of him and worried about his devastated reaction to the break-up. She was better able to take care of herself with the coordinated efforts of her parents, her friends, her school and the police.[1]

There are cases in which the only way to end the violence after the relationship is over is for the family to take extreme measures to get the battered teen completely away from the batterer. These kinds of measures are especially necessary when the batterer's threats or behavior indicate that it is possible he will try to kill his ex-girlfriend or someone in her family. If he is part of a gang or is otherwise known to be capable of murder, these measures are absolutely necessary and must be quickly decided.

She may have to hide, changing her school and residence. She may try to stay in one of the shelters for battered women which have been established for this purpose. Some of them accept teens, and some cities have shelters for teens. She may have to leave town for a while, sometimes for a long time, staying with relatives or family friends. She may have to keep her new residence a secret from school, friends and others so that it will not be inadvertently revealed to the batterer.

In some cases, the whole family must move to another city without leaving a forwarding address. Occasionally, the family must also change their name and take detailed precautions so that the batterer does not find out where they are living.

The process of breaking up is very complicated in these situations. Planning to break up may take considerable time and effort so that the batterer does not suspect that his girlfriend is thinking of leaving. The family must make detailed plans for her to disappear suddenly, so that when he finds out that she has left, and he explodes with violence, he cannot find her.

For teen mothers whose batterer is the father of their child or children, this can be especially complicated because of legal issues regarding the custody and visitation of the child. It might take some preparation to plan to leave town with the child.

Emotional Reactions After Breaking Up

You can help your daughter anticipate her feelings about being apart from her batterer when she breaks up with him. What will she need? Will she want to be physically far away from him so that she can't see him (even by accident), to avoid feeling pressured by him or having her own feelings pull her back to him? Will she want to be with other people most of the time? Will she want to be at home and doing her usual routine? Will she need help from others to keep her from having any contact with him?

Most people leaving a battering relationship are vulnerable to going back, especially about two weeks to two months after breaking up. This is a critical time. It is not a matter of how much time it takes to get over the relationship, but of getting through the times when your daughter feels the pull back to him. Your daughter needs continuous support. You cannot assume that her need for your support is over because the relationship is over. Quite the contrary: She will still be emotionally vulnerable, and possibly in physical danger, for a long time after the break-up.

After things quiet down, and she has become involved in a new routine that doesn't focus on her relationship, she will feel the pull to go back. She will start missing the things that were good in the relationship, and minimizing the bad times. She will feel bad about how much the batterer may be suffering or despairing or missing her. She will experience the fear and intense pain of being alone, which is especially acute after the intense demands of a battering relationship. She will be afraid of what the batterer will do, and the tension can be unbearable. She might seek the relief of staying close, watching, accommodating him, feeling like she is managing the situation when she is in contact with him rather than coping with the fear of the unknown when she is apart from him.

Now that her boyfriend is not around, your daughter may be experiencing intense feelings she could not feel when she was with him. She may be depressed, even thinking of suicide. She may be angry with herself, and afraid to trust herself in the future. Her self-esteem has been seriously undermined, and she may be having a hard time believing that she can get over this, or do better on her own, or do the things she wants to do. She may be terrified, realizing what she has been through. She may feel ashamed and guilty, realizing what her family has been through. She may be angry, realizing how badly she has been treated, or how unsupportive some people have been.

Your daughter needs support to overcome the isolation she experienced during the relationship. She has to re-establish friendships and fill the gaps left by the batterer in her social and emotional life. She needs to be embraced by her family. Family members have also been affected by the violence. This is a time of healing and restoration for all of you.

Your daughter needs help from you and from people at her school to regain lost ground, academically, socially and in her other activities. She needs counseling to help her recover her self-esteem, and to deal with the intense push and pull to and from the battering relationship. She needs counseling to recover from the traumatic effects of the relationship, to evaluate what she has been through, how it has affected her and how to believe in herself again.

Considerations if the Batterer Stops the Violence

So far we have focused on continued battering or on the break-up with a batterer who has gotten worse, not better. However, in some cases the person who is violent realizes he has a problem, and gets help to stop his violence. There are several common motivations for a batterer to make a change like this. He may be afraid he'll lose the relationship. He may realize he has an alcohol or drug problem, get sober or clean, and find out he can control his violent behavior. He may get arrested, severely injure his girlfriend or lose access to his child, or for some other reason be forced to face the reality of the consequences of his violent behavior. He may be court-ordered into a counseling program, and learn he can change the way he treats his girlfriend. Something might change for him, on his own or in the relationship, and a long period might go by during which he finds he can calm himself and prevent his violent explosions. The change can be permanent.

The longer and more frequently batterers have used violence in the past, the harder it is to give it up. For this reason, teens have a better chance of stopping their violent behavior than do older people. Stopping one's own violence means being constantly aware of your own potential to use violence—in your current relationship or in any other relationship in the future. Batterers must take responsibility for handling situations, circumstances or conditions that might trigger their violence.

Because of the possibility that he could resort to violence again, you and your daughter and her boyfriend will need to keep the same safety plans in place. This is not to minimize his accomplishments in controlling his violence. Rather this is to provide a realistic support system that reduces the risk that he will disappoint everyone and hurt his girlfriend by using violence again.

If you are the parent of a battered teen whose batterer has recognized the seriousness of his problem with violence, and has changed, how are you affected?

First, before assuming that the violence has stopped, continue to check out the possibility that it might have become hidden.

If the violence has stopped and the couple continue to see each other, you may feel relieved that things have changed for the better. You may find that when your daughter's boyfriend has his violence under control, he can be a pleasure to have around. But what if you don't feel relieved, and continue to feel uneasy? Do you notice that although the physical violence has stopped, the other patterns in the relationship continue to be the same? While you are relieved that your daughter is not being beaten, are you concerned that she is still being emotionally abused or sexually assaulted? Your daughter and her boyfriend may be experiencing an extended reconciliation within the cycle of violence. Or, the physical abuse might have stopped but the same cycle of violence continues, with emotional and, possibly, sexual abuse. If this is the case, your daughter continues to be in an abusive relationship. As we discussed earlier in this book, emotional abuse is also a serious problem, and can have a devastating effect on its victims.

This does not mean that batterers can't stop being violent. It means that they must continue to be aware of their feelings and the circumstances around them so that they can deal with the feelings and situations that arise in alternative, non-violent ways. He can establish prevention strategies for himself, such as people to call or a place to go to cool off if he feels explosive.

He may find counseling helpful to support these changes. Even if specialized help is not available, most cities have counseling programs. Group counseling can be especially effective. Alcoholics Anonymous and other self-help support groups assist with accountability and conscientiousness in maintaining changes. The next chapter provides more information about counseling resources.

8

USING COMMUNITY RESOURCES: COUNSELING, SCHOOLS AND THE LEGAL SYSTEM

Counseling

Jane, seventeen years old:

> It wasn't until I went to see a counselor that I understood what had been happening to me. It took some time, but I was able to figure out why I was still so hooked on Peter. Even after all the ways he tortured me and hurt me, and I knew I didn't want to be with him any more, I couldn't stop thinking about him. My counselor helped me see that because of being battered I was focused on him so much I couldn't take care of myself. I became stronger, I wasn't so afraid any more, and I even felt happy, having fun with friends again like I hadn't for two years.

Jane's mother, Sheila:

> I was as angry at Jane as I was at her boyfriend! I didn't trust her because she had lied to me so many times. She said she was getting stronger, and wouldn't lie to me about seeing him again, but I kept watching and accusing her. Finally, I went to a few counseling sessions with Jane. I came to understand

what had happened to her and why she cut me off when she was close to her boyfriend. I also realized that I was angry with Jane because I was so afraid that I would lose her. Now I don't get as angry, and I can listen better. We're beginning to rebuild our trust.

Counseling can make a difference as a way for you and/or your daughter to sort out feelings, to think about how to deal with the situation and to gain emotional support. Individual counseling, support groups and family counseling are all very helpful. Counseling by specialists in domestic violence is available through domestic violence shelters and counseling programs. Most states and cities have rape and/or domestic violence hotlines that make referrals to individual specialists and support groups who specialize in dealing with domestic violence.

Groups are especially valuable for dealing with dating violence. It helps to hear other teens' or other parents' experiences, including those of others who have not left their batterers. It helps to hear different perspectives on a problem that everyone in the group has experienced. It is comforting and supportive to find that you are not isolated, and that other people have had similar problems.

Many battered women's shelters have weekly "drop-in" support groups that are open to community members on an as-needed basis. Even though these groups are not usually geared to teens, many teens have found them helpful. Some domestic violence programs have groups for teens; these are extremely helpful. Drop-in groups have the advantage of being available with no pressure, because you can attend whenever you want to. Other kinds of groups are offered for a particular period of time, for example, once a week for 10 weeks, and you make a commitment to attend consistently during that time. Everyone starts and ends at the same time. Still others are ongoing, but require an intake interview and a commitment to attend regularly. Rather than different people attending the group each time, as in a drop-in group, the same group members get to know one another. People leave the group as they feel they are ready to move on.

Sometimes, when the violence of the situation is serious, a teen has to get to a safe place. For example, if the batterer is threatening her (and/or others close to her) with physical harm and is known to be capable of inflicting harm, and there is no other safe place for her to stay, you should call a shelter for battered women. Find out if the shelter nearest you accepts teens into their program. Some do. If it doesn't, you may have to go to a shelter that is not in your area or find another kind of refuge with the help of your local shelter. A shelter offers a safe, hidden refuge along with counseling and advocacy services for planning future safety.

Counseling is also available through mental health centers, family service agencies, and general counseling programs as well as various kinds of youth programs. Some youth programs, such as YM/YWCAs, community centers, recreation centers, athletic programs, neighborhood youth centers and gang services, have special programs to help young people deal with relationships, sexuality, and issues of violence. Teen mother programs have support groups that deal with relationship and parenting issues, including violence. We have found excellent services for teens dealing with violent relationships in programs for pregnant and parenting teens.

Health clinics that serve young people can be a helpful resource. They often offer services for runaways or other high-risk teens, some of whom have had violent dating experiences. A call to a teen health clinic can be helpful because the staff may be able to offer suggestions for resources for teens and can be a support to parents who are stressed. You may also use one of these clinics for health care to treat injuries caused by battering.

Some people find additional help in their religious communities. Ministers, rabbis, priests, nuns and other religious leaders can be supportive. A teen who is involved in a youth group may find the group leader to be a source of support: for example, the leader may be able to encourage the teen's continued involvement in the group as she struggles with her batterer's attempts to isolate her. If both partners of the couple are part of the same church or youth group, leaders and everyone in that environment can be actively involved in her safety and in getting the batterer to acknowledge that he has a problem and needs help. Teens have told us about abusive incidents that have taken place in church when other people were around. Church members and leaders can be alert, talking openly with the couple or with the abused teen to find out what is going on and to intervene.

Counseling for batterers should be more comprehensive than just groups or anger control or conflict resolution classes. These are helpful in conjunction with individual or group batterer treatment programs. But treatment programs should offer a more in-depth psycho-educational approach to the problem, with accountability for violent behavior built into the program. The batterer's counseling program should maintain contact with the victim if the couple is still in a relationship, as a source of accurate information about the batterer's current abusive behavior, and to ensure the safety of the victim.

Counseling for your daughter and her boyfriend as a couple is not advised until the batterer's verbal abuse and physical violence have stopped. Otherwise the counseling sessions can be intimidating or even dangerous experiences for the battered teen. However, counseling as a couple can be helpful for the parents.

When you look for a counselor, there are several criteria you can use to select someone to help with dating violence. Look for a counselor who has experience in dealing with domestic violence. One way to do this is to ask for referrals from your local domestic violence program or hotline.

In the initial interview to assess the problem, your daughter must feel safe in describing her actual experiences. The counselor should not ask your daughter to discuss the relationship or the violence in the presence of the batterer.

Questions to ask a counselor you are considering seeing include:

- Do you have expertise in domestic violence? Have you ever worked with someone who has been abused or raped in a relationship? What kind of training do you have in this work?
- What techniques do you use in working with battered teens or teen batterers?
- Do you recommend counseling as a couple when there is abuse in the relationship?
- Would you support my participation in a group?
- How would you deal with the ongoing threat of violence toward me and/or my daughter?
- Are you available in emergencies? How can you be reached?

Schools as a Resource

If your daughter and/or her abuser are junior high/middle school, high school or college students, you can enlist the school's support in planning for your daughter's safety. School personnel can be a source of information about what is actually happening if you do not have a clear picture of the extent of the violence. They can be a source of current information as the situation changes, and participate in a safety net for your daughter. Schools have the resources and authority to influence the batterer to stop his violence.

Your daughter might not like your contacting her school or your "interference" (as she might see it). She might protect her boyfriend from intervention by the school, or deny that she is being battered to school personnel who try to discuss the problem with her. When dealing with dating violence, parents often, as we have discussed earlier, have to make decisions to take actions based on concern for their child's safety at the risk of making their child angry or withdrawn from them.

Schools and individuals within school systems vary tremendously in how helpful they are or are willing to be. They may be unwilling to intervene in what they may consider a family problem or a problem for which they don't have policies or protocols requiring them to take action. Most often they don't know how to intervene, but are otherwise willing to work with parents. Your approach will vary accordingly.

Establish contact with someone at your daughter's school by calling or visiting the principal or vice principal, the counselor, the nurse, security staff, or a particular teacher who knows and has a relationship with your child. If someone from the school contacts you because of your child's absence or another problem, use the opportunity to talk with them about how your child is doing, and to alert them to the violence. You can also ask for information about your child, and about the batterer if he goes to the same school. It might be helpful for you to find out about your daughter's attendance and how school personnel see her. For example, have they noticed any changes in her behavior or academic status, observed any incidents of abuse, or heard about violence toward her from other students?

The school can help by taking action directly with your daughter's abuser. For example, if he is not a student, he should not be on campus. School personnel who are aware of the problem can make sure he does not come onto or near the campus. If he is a student, you can find out what policies the school has regarding action its staff can and will take to protect your daughter from being abused while at school.

The school's cooperation can be especially helpful in planning for your daughter's safety. School personnel can watch out for her, separate her from the abuser if he is bothering her at school, or call you if she needs help. Often school personnel do not call parents with a problem of this sort, but they might be more likely to do so if you alert them to the seriousness of the problem and let them know that you want to be informed and you want to work with them. Schools are unpredictable, and you may get a cooperative response or you may get an apathetic or resistant one. You might try approaching different people at the school until you connect with a responsive person: for example, if the vice principal isn't helpful, try talking to the counselor or the nurse.

Some parents have changed their daughter's school to get her away from her batterer. Other parents have arranged to drop their daughters off and pick them up from school, to minimize her contact with her boyfriend. These actions have had mixed results, depending on the situation. If your daughter is not ready to break up, she may fight the change, find other ways to see him, or drop out of school or not attend regularly ("ditch"). On the other hand, this approach may actually make it harder for him to see her, which could be a relief for her if she is ambivalent or if she is ready to be out from under his daily control at school.

Learning About School Policies

Your child's high school or college may call the police or campus security if a violent incident takes place at school. The school may have a policy requiring a report to the parents, or they may have no policies at all. They may have protocols for how to respond to relationship violence that takes place on or near campus. They may require disciplinary action, a visit to a counselor or a call to the police. If your children's schools have not developed any protocols for dealing with these situations, you may want to pressure them to do so.

Recently, some schools have developed protocols for handling violence between students and sexual harassment on campus. Although not intended to address relationship violence, these protocols can be used by your child's school to deal with battering, especially if the batterer attends the same school. In California, a recent law making it a felony to commit assault against anyone on school campuses can be used to restrain violent dating partners.

Violence Prevention Programs

Local domestic violence and rape crisis organizations may have a prevention education and/or counseling program at the school. Other organizations such as Planned Parenthood and some substance abuse programs, conduct workshops in schools on issues related to dating and to sexual or dating violence. You may be able to contact one of these programs directly about ways to get help for your daughter. Even when you are not ready to use services they offer, knowing about them will help you be prepared when ready. These school-affiliated programs may offer resources for your daughter that do not directly relate to her battering but that will help her build her strengths and support networks outside her relationship.

School-Based Services

Check out other resources that may be provided within the high school or college. Many schools have support groups related to various personal or school-related problems, such as drop-out prevention, substance abuse and pregnant teen groups in high schools, and stress groups in college counseling centers. A school counselor or nurse might refer your daughter to one of these support groups. Many schools have health clinics that offer group or individual counseling. Many schools have Alcoholics Anonymous or Alateen program meetings for students, which might be a good resource for your daughter.

If your daughter attends college, there may be several options for making help available to her on campus. Many schools have Women's Resource Centers with libraries, workshops, discussion groups, or drop-in centers where young women can hang out and talk. Most colleges have counseling departments or psychology services where students can obtain group or individual counseling for free or for a very low fee. Larger colleges have student health services that provide basic health care to students for free or at minimal cost. Health clinics may provide opportunities for your daughter to talk privately with a nurse or a nurse practitioner, or they may provide counseling.

If your daughter lives on campus in a dormitory or another officially supervised residence, there is usually a dormitory advisor or house mother whose job it is to talk with students about problems they face. Some schools have peer counseling programs; others have student advisors or academic advisors assigned to each student who are available and can help. College rape prevention and sexual harassment prevention programs are good resources for information, referrals and peer counseling.

Using the Legal System

> The law is a tool to stop battering. [Legal action] can empower the victim of domestic violence and let her know she doesn't have to deal with the violence all by herself; at the same time it sends a powerful message to the batterer: The state government knows what you are doing and it not only disapproves but will punish you as well. Once a victim takes that first step to tell someone about the violence and ask for help, she may use the law to aid her in escaping the violence. However, as you might expect, the law has its limits.[1]

The legal system includes law enforcement, prosecution, court, probation and parole systems. You may have contact with any or all of these systems in dealing with teen dating violence. Laws, regulations and procedures vary from one city, county, and state to another, so you will need to find out what to expect of the legal system in your area.[2]

There are two parallel systems of law that address domestic violence. Criminal law reflects those actions defined by the legislature as a crime for which a person can be prosecuted by a state or a local prosecutor. Civil law involves a person suing another to obtain some kind of court order or judgment. Different kinds of courts handle the different kinds of claims:

criminal courts hear criminal matters, and juvenile courts hear criminal matters in which a minor is accused. A variety of civil courts hear matters including divorces, adoptions and most domestic violence restraining-order cases.

In most courts, a minor (defined as someone under the age of eighteen) does not have legal status. A minor can file a police complaint, and can testify as a witness in a criminal case. A minor cannot usually file a civil case or ask for a restraining order unless he or she has a *guardian ad litem* (guardian for the purpose of litigation) to appear with them in court. The *guardian ad litem* can be any adult (for example, a parent or a counselor) who fills out a form requesting to be appointed guardian and who files the order or the case on behalf of the minor.

In most states, restraining orders or specific laws criminalizing domestic violence are not available to anyone under eighteen. In addition, most domestic violence laws do not include dating relationships in the definition of domestic violence, even for adults. Other, more general laws may be involved in domestic violence cases.

If a victim of dating violence reports the battering to the police, even if the relationship is not covered by laws criminalizing domestic violence, the abuser may be charged with other crimes. Most states have the following crimes on the books:

Criminal harassment: subjecting another to physical contact, following them around or phoning them continually if it is done with the *intent* to harass, alarm or annoy them, if it has that *effect* or if the behavior occurs with *no legitimate purpose*.

Reckless endangerment: placing a person in serious risk of bodily injury or death.

Assault: intentionally or negligently causing or attempting to cause bodily injury.

Aggravated assault: intentionally or negligently causing or attempting to cause grave injury, as with a weapon.

You should be aware that the police can arrest someone suspected of felony criminal behavior if they have "probable cause" to believe that person has committed the crime. At the misdemeanor level, an officer must actually see the behavior in order to make an arrest. Some states specifically allow probable-cause arrests in domestic violence. Generally, arrest is discretionary. Some local law enforcement agencies, such as the Los Angeles Police Department, have adopted mandatory arrest policies for domestic violence cases, requiring police officers to make an arrest when they see evidence of physical injury.

Restraining Orders

Every state has some form of statutory law that defines the kinds of relationships and restraining orders covered by civil laws governing domestic violence. Under these laws, a person who has been battered by family members or someone who fits a certain category of intimacy can petition a court for a number of different orders that restrain the behavior of the batterer for a short time (a temporary order) or a longer time (an order after a hearing, or a "permanent" order, whose duration can vary).

A temporary order, obtained in an emergency situation by going to a court without notice to the batterer, usually lasts one to two weeks. Then there must be a hearing before the order is continued. Permanent orders vary in duration, and can be for six months, one year or three years. There are several kinds of permanent orders: "keep-away" orders ordering a batterer to stay away from the victim's home, place of work or school; orders requiring a batterer to leave the family of the victim alone or to stop telephoning; and orders affecting the custody of children or the division of certain kinds of property.

In order to obtain one of these orders, a teenage victim or the *guardian ad litem* must file a request with the appropriate civil court. In most states these orders are heard in the same court as divorces, but in some states and counties, there may be a separate courtroom just for domestic violence order applications, or they may be heard in a more general civil court. A restraining order must always be served on the person whose behavior is being restrained before it becomes effective. In most states, the police, marshals or deputies provide service of process for a small fee. In some states the victim is allowed to serve the papers herself, but should be accompanied by a law enforcement officer for safety reasons. If the batterer attends the same school, school authorities should be notified of the existence of the restraining order.

The violation of civil domestic violence restraining orders is a crime. Teens who violate orders may be brought to juvenile court, where penalties vary. For example, they may be sentenced to juvenile detention, ordered to pay a fine or given alternative sentencing like counseling or attending a school different from the victim's.

Teenage victims have the option of obtaining restraining orders under the state's civil harassment laws if they do not qualify under the state's domestic violence laws. These laws cover violence or annoyance between strangers, neighbors or co-workers. The clerk of your local court should be able to provide the forms required for all the applicable restraining orders.

Some dating violence victims may not want to get restraining orders because of fear that the batterer will become angry. This may be true, but it may also have an impact on the batterer to know that he could be arrested for harassing, threatening or being violent towards the victim.

Some teens who are battered fear the orders are just pieces of paper that do not stop the batterers. Restraining orders are only as good as the batterer's willingness to comply with them for fear of being arrested. For many, that fear serves as an effective restraint; for others, it doesn't. In addition, when a victim holds a restraining order, enforcement possibilities are enhanced when the police are called to respond to a threat of violence. Police can make an arrest for a violation of a restraining order whereas they cannot make an arrest for threatened violence if no crime has yet been committed or they have seen no evidence that it was committed.

Calling the Police

Calling the police can be an important safety mechanism when violence takes place. Like a restraining order, a police report can be a deterrent for batterers who are afraid of arrest and jail. Intervention by police conveys a powerful message to the batterer that his actions are criminal and can lead to his arrest. Many teen batterers are shocked to find out that hitting their girlfriends is illegal, and their perspectives change when they see the consequences of their behavior. Reporting to the police also conveys a powerful message to the teen who is being abused: she doesn't have to deal with the violence all by herself.

Previous exposure to the criminal justice system makes a difference in whether or not a teen batterer will be deterred by being arrested. If he has already been arrested for drug abuse or dealing, gang affiliations or other problems, two reactions are common: first, he is more likely to be arrested and spend time in jail for battering because of his prior record; and second, he is less likely to be intimidated by the threat of arrest. Of course, there are many exceptions—for example, if the teen is on parole or probation and trying to stay out of trouble.

Even in situations when the police find they do not have enough information to make an arrest, they can file a report that can be useful in documenting a pattern of violence or can later be used to help obtain a restraining order.

Stalking—What You Can Do About It

Stalking is now illegal in most states. The police can be called to report a boyfriend or ex-boyfriend who is continually following your daughter, calling constantly, sending letters, threatening her or your family, destroying property, or showing up at school or at work to harass or intimidate her.

California law defines stalking as willful, malicious, and repeated following or harassment that presents a credible threat, with the intent to place the victim in reasonable fear for his or her safety or the safety of his or her immediate family. Stalking consists of a pattern or a series of acts over a period of time, however short. The conduct is directed at a particular person, "seriously alarms, annoys, torments, or terrorizes the person" and serves no legitimate purpose.

Call your local police department to find out what constitutes stalking according to the law in your city, county or state. Find out what procedures are necessary to report stalking. Then follow the procedures that will make police and legal intervention possible.

The Los Angeles Police Department recommends that you keep a written record of every incident or contact with the stalker. Keep tape recordings of threatening messages left on your answering machine, labeled with the dates and times of the calls. The LAPD also recommends reporting the stalking to the police so that they are aware of what is going on. In addition, you should obtain a restraining order as a deterrent and as documentation of the behavior. You can then report the violation of the restraining order if the stalking continues.

Reporting and Prosecuting Sexual Assault

Reporting sexual assault is an option for teens and their parents. However, parents will find it frustrating to report a sexual assault unless they have their daughter's cooperation. District attorneys cannot prosecute without a cooperative witness, especially in cases of date or acquaintance rape.

Some parents have reported batterers who are over eighteen for statutory rape of their daughters who are minors. If your minor daughter has been sexually assaulted but doesn't want to make a police report, and you feel strongly about reporting it, talk to your local detective about the option of making a statutory rape filing.

If you and your daughter are attempting to prosecute a batterer for physical assault, you can add sexual assault to the other violent behavior being addressed in the case. Sometimes sexual assault will be taken more seriously when considered in the context of repeated violence.

Although prosecuting sexual assault is an arduous process, many teens feel strengthened by pursuing this option, seeing it as part of their healing. Others have found it traumatic (and revictimizing) to undergo repeated questioning about their experience. It is more difficult to undergo questioning about sexual assault than about physical assault or other crimes.

9

CULTURAL STRENGTHS
AND CHALLENGES

The values and beliefs of your culture or your religion may affect your feelings and your family's response to your daughter's abusive relationship. Therefore, you must consider your values and beliefs in making assessments and decisions about your daughter's situation. Sometimes these cultural influences are barriers to a family's effectiveness by limiting understanding, objectivity and options. Other times, cultural traditions provide resources to the family for support.

Cultural Influences

Cultural values and beliefs about relationships, dating, marriage, sex and seeking help influence your family's way of dealing with your daughter's situation. The values of your culture may require marriage to the person she has sex with or, if she is pregnant, to the father of her child. This presents a conflict for you if you are also worried about a marriage filled with violence.

Your cultural views about dating affect how you react to

dating violence. Your family may prohibit dating or prescribe certain rules about it. This may lead your daughter to keep her dating activities hidden from you. You may feel angry that she has violated your values, and then, more angry to discover she has also been hurt by the person she is dating.

Your options for taking action will be limited if you believe that women must support the men in their lives because they have been discriminated against. This can create conflict between your dual allegiances. Your choices may also be affected by the belief that women are responsible for the problems that arise in intimate relationships.

Your values and beliefs about what constitutes a serious problem will affect how you react. If your family or community has experienced tremendous trauma, change or distress, your daughter's problems with her boyfriend may not be seen as serious. For example, many communities, such as those from Armenia, Cambodia and El Salvador, have experienced genocidal massacres or torture during war, or very difficult journeys as immigrants or refugees. Having survived enormous tragedies affects how you respond to crises that arise in your family life. You may expect your daughter to tolerate or resign herself to this way of life.

It is often difficult in an oppressed community to reveal violence or any other problem that contradicts the image of the culture as being free of such problems. For example, Jewish cultural attitudes hide family violence as a *shanda* (shame). Asian-Americans are seen as a "model minority," which may lead to the desired invisibility of problems such as family violence. African-American families are often reluctant to report family violence because of a sense of shame and their vulnerability to discrimination based on racism.

Building on Cultural Strengths

Culture and traditions provide strength to families and individuals. The culture in which we have grown up affects our beliefs, values, behavior and how we deal with problems. Therefore, we are all different in terms of what will be effective for each of us and each of our families in dealing with interpersonal violence. Our culture, ethnic group, religion, and economic background all contribute to forming a complicated set of influences, constraints and resources.

We often rely on our cultural traditions for sanctuary and support. They offer us ways of seeing our problems so that we feel comforted and able to understand what is happening to us. They offer us communities with shared values in which we maintain a sense of belonging and connection. They offer ancestral and collective histories which form and inform our identities. We benefit from rituals and traditions that help us move from one phase of life to another. We use prayers for healing. We find resources in our cultural communities that help us solve problems. We seek support from religious and spiritual leaders, teachers and guides.

Legal definitions of what constitutes abuse have recently changed in the United States. Abuse is now defined in terms of the people who have been abused, which has challenged the perception and acceptance of abuse as an invisible and normal part of life. There has been a social revolution affecting institutions that relied upon the "normalcy" of certain aspects of family life—for example, methods of disciplining children, rights of husbands and fathers to control their families, and courtship practices. Previously unquestioned authority is being challenged. Girls have new rights. They don't have to accept abuse in their relationships.

The changing roles and status of women and girls in the

United States have presented challenges and provoked conflict within cultures, communities and families. In families that have recently immigrated to the United States, parents often form a bridge from the old to the new, wanting better lives for their children. They do not want them to experience limitations that they themselves experienced in their own countries or cultures of origin. Forming this bridge is complicated and difficult. But parents must make choices, and even if those choices conflict with cultural or religious values, they are important for the protection and safety of our children. Changing beliefs means taking risks.

The following are examples of beliefs related to family violence that exist in some cultures, including the dominant culture in this country:

- A woman must marry the man who raped her.
- A woman must stay in a marriage in which she is beaten.
- A husband has a right to beat his wife.
- Hitting or beating children to control their behavior is an effective form of discipline.
- Courtship must lead to marriage, or girls must marry the husband that parents select or prefer.
- Young people must wait until marriage to have sexually intimate relationships.

Confronting Your Culture

People in conflict within their cultures and between cultures must make choices. Using culture as an excuse when in conflict is avoiding responsibility. If you say, "He or she behaves violently because of their culture," or "In our religion, she must marry him since she is with him, even if he hits her," you make the culture responsible for the violence, rather than holding individuals responsible for their choices. It is important to challenge such beliefs and to hold people who are violent accountable and responsible for their choices about using violence, whether or not the culture or social environment tolerates it. If you challenge such beliefs, you are less likely to "blame the victim." When you actively intervene on your daughter's behalf, she knows that she has the right to be treated with respect, that she doesn't deserve to be abused, that abuse is never acceptable—in any culture.

Culture influences decisions to take action and what kind of action to take, including where to go for help. Your decisions about seeking help from schools, the legal system, friends or family depend on what fits with your values, beliefs and the resources within your culture and your community.

Supports that are available within your culture can be helpful and empowering. You can expect understanding, trust, familiarity. Seeking help within your community may be necessary because of expectations or experiences of criticism, judgmental responses, or discrimination outside the community. Language can be a barrier to seeking help outside the community. Your language and communication style may be misunderstood, especially if English is not your primary language and your ability to communicate is affected by stress. Your cultural values may emphasize helping people within your own community, and your community may offer resources for personal support. For example, in the African-American community, church and civil rights organizations provide a wide variety of services. Culturally-sensitive services are available in many cities—for example, Asian Service Centers, Armenian school-based centers, Jewish Family Services, and Spanish-speaking shelters for Latinas who have been battered.

Seeking help within the community can have problems as well. In a closed community, privacy is limited. Cultural values lead to feelings of shame about yourself and your family if a relationship problem is revealed, especially a problem such as sexual violence.

If you have recently arrived in the United States, you face the enormous task of learning how this country's laws, institutions and policies work, and what to expect. Getting help or planning for your child's safety means learning new methods or dealing with those that are different from what is familiar to you and your family.

Repeated experiences with discrimination may affect your willingness to rely on institutions. For example, an African-American teen who expects her boyfriend to be arrested, jailed and possibly treated badly may be reluctant to call the police or reveal that she is battered to anyone outside her community.

Discrimination based on stereotyped expectations and misperceptions of your behavior can lead to your being misunderstood. For example, if your culture and customs make it unacceptable for you to tell strangers about personal problems, your difficulty talking to a helping person might be misunderstood as unwillingness to cooperate. Lack of communication can lead to your being judged, blamed or criticized for your behavior when seeking help. People who are supposed to help can sometimes be insensitive, but they may have useful resources to offer you.

As parents, all of us find ourselves confronting the ways in which we grew up differently from our children. Our children constantly remind us that "It's different now, not the way it was back then." Some of us look to cultural traditions for perspectives on what is happening with our children, others do not. But it is important for all of us to find new ways to support our children as they deal with the realities of their lives.

10

FOR PARENTS OF GAY, LESBIAN OR BISEXUAL TEENS

Jeffrey's Story

My name is Jeffrey, and I just turned twenty-one. I was eighteen years old when I started dating Bob, who was twenty-eight. I lived with my mother, and I knew I couldn't tell her about my relationship with Bob. There were no other adults in my life. We lived in a small town far away from the rest of the family. Mostly, I talked to my straight friends in high school. I was the only out person, and my friends were very accepting of me.

Bob was abusive. It was psychological at first, then it became physical. He dominated me. I was mentally brainwashed. There were certain things I couldn't do because if I did I was in big trouble. If he was supposed to pick me up at seven, I had to be ready at 7:00, not 6:55 or 7:05, or he'd explode. If he didn't like what I was wearing, he'd tell me all day how awful I looked. I tried very hard not to make him angry. After a while, I fought back verbally, and I harped on him. When he would hit me, I'd fight back, get a few punches in. I wouldn't just stand there and let a man hit me. But he was bigger and older than me, and it would escalate. It didn't do any good to defend myself physically. Several times, I called the police. They didn't do anything. I thought they were making fun of me.

My mom was into her own stuff. She was dating, and got married. She was busy. She didn't want to believe I was gay. She saw me with a black eye, and thought something must have happened in school. So she asked me, "How was school?" I said, "You don't want to know." And she didn't. She never tried to find out. She knows now, but she doesn't want to talk about it. We get along OK. We don't see each other too much.

My friends were the ones who helped me get away from Bob. They understood me and validated me. They didn't put words in my mouth. No "you should" or "you have to." They helped me think about my options. They asked me, "Do you like being a slave? Do you like being punched and battered?" I got the message. They told me it was my decision. I am very grateful to them. With my friends' support, I got strong enough to pull away and eventually break up with Bob. Bob kept pursuing me. So I got a restraining order, and he finally stayed away.

This illustrates the painful reality for teens who cannot share important aspects of their lives (for example, whom they love) with their parents, and therefore cannot approach their parents when they need support to deal with dating violence.

Parents are often surprised to find that teens can be in gay and lesbian relationships, and that battering can take place in those relationships. Most of these teens do not tell their parents about their relationships or the battering. When teens are not being open about who they are dating, they are more likely to keep problems with violence a secret. They are also more likely to keep their relationships secret from their peers. The fear of homophobic reactions from parents, peers and others results in isolation. So your teen may have no one to confide in about a problem with violence.

In addition to being isolated, gay and lesbian teen relationships are often "invisible." Parents, friends and other people don't notice the warning signs of abuse or violence because they don't notice the relationship. If your teen is bisexual, and dating both boys and girls, you may know nothing about the same sex relationship. People who assume that everyone is heterosexual do not consider the possibility that two girls or two boys may be intensely involved or in love.

Parents often have difficulty recognizing and accepting that their child might be gay, lesbian or bisexual. It is understandable that many teens keep their gay relationships secret. They are afraid of being rejected, abused or humiliated. Teens have been thrown out by their families or have run away because of parents' severe reactions to their homosexuality.

Marion's Story

Marion noticed that her seventeen-year-old daughter, Suzanne, was beginning to change.

Suzanne was spending more and more time with her best friend, Melissa. They were inseparable. I noticed that they were fighting a lot. Suzanne would come home late, after her curfew, usually in tears. Then she wouldn't get up in the morning until just as I was leaving for work. I suspected that she wasn't going to school, so I called and found out she was absent ten days that month and had been forging my signature on notes.

I confronted her about school. I was already worried about this friendship because she was constantly upset, and now this. I told her I thought Melissa was a bad influence on her. Suzanne promised to straighten things out with Melissa and not to miss any more school.

About a month later, we were shopping for clothes and I noticed bruises on her arm and scratches on her back. I was alarmed and asked her, "Who did this to you?!" Suzanne then told me that Melissa was more than a friend: They had been "involved" for six months. Suzanne said she was in love with her, but Melissa got drunk and jealous and pushed her around.

This whole thing was very hard for me. I didn't know what to think. She was so unhappy. I didn't know if it was just Melissa, or if this was what her life was going to be.

The night that Suzanne came home with bruises on her face, I wasn't confused any more. I told her, "This is getting worse. You need help." She told me, sobbing, that she had been trying to break up with Melissa. Then I realized that Suzanne was trapped: She couldn't get away from her. I'd heard about this with married couples, but at her age! And with a girl! This I couldn't believe. So I started getting information. She needed my help. No one could tell me about girls who batter other girls, but I found out what we needed to do. Suzanne was torn, afraid to hurt Melissa, but she was so relieved to have some support to get out of the relationship.

Now I see Suzanne with another girlfriend, a really lovely girl. I don't know if she's going to want this—what is the word?—"lifestyle" for the rest of her life. Maybe she can be happy, but I'm sure glad she had the strength to get away from Melissa.

The patterns in violent gay relationships are similar to those in violent straight relationships. They consist of emotionally, physically and sexually violent behavior. The cycle of violence is the same. The motivation behind the use of violence by gay or lesbian batterers, as with straight batterers, is to maintain power and control over the other person.

A bisexual teen who batters usually acts differently with a gay or lesbian partner. For example, a bisexual boy or girl may be abusive towards a gay or lesbian partner, but not towards a heterosexual one. Occasionally, girls who have been abused by boys or men are abusive towards their girlfriends. Some bisexual teens find more intensity in their same-sex relationships than in their straight relationships. Sometimes this intensity involves jealousy and restrictive, controlling behavior as well as violence.

The isolation that is so often part of any battering situation is complicated and worsened by the isolation imposed by the secrecy of a gay relationship. The battering gay relationship also becomes insular as the couple keeps their secrets, and as they rely more and more on each other to defend themselves against anyone finding out about them. In addition, to control his or her boyfriend or girlfriend, a gay batterer may threaten to tell others about their relationship.

Sometimes teens feel that they are being punished because they are gay, lesbian or bisexual, and feel that they deserve the abuse. This makes them vulnerable and traps them in the abusive relationship.

Gay teens often have few norms or role models for their relationships, which is confusing for them. They may assume that the abuse is a normal part of all gay and lesbian relationships until they have more exposure to healthy relationships.

Teens going through the process of coming out commonly have mixed feelings about themselves and how they fit in socially. They tend to struggle with denial about being gay or lesbian, feel socially isolated, despise themselves, hide their true feelings from others, and live in fear of rejection and violence. It becomes even harder for teens to develop positive feelings about their gay or lesbian identities while being hit, manipulated and emotionally battered in a relationship that is part of their gay experience.

Parents have their own issues to confront about their teen's gay or lesbian relationships. Like Marion, you may only find out that your teen is gay, lesbian or bisexual when you find out about the abuse. Then your reactions to learning both "secrets" at the same time become intertwined. Some parents react with negativity about gay relationships, assuming that by nature they are dangerous or dysfunctional. You may not take your teen's relationship seriously, seeing it as a "phase" that he or she will outgrow.

You might focus on your teen's homosexuality rather than the abuse, trying to change your teen's sexual orientation rather than helping him or her deal with the violence. For example, when sixteen-year-old Elizabeth was stressed or bruised, her family wondered out loud why she put up with her friend's bullying. But they never asked about the relationship or confronted the violence until her father found a love letter Elizabeth's girlfriend had written to her. Then they became furious, punished her, and forbade her from seeing her girlfriend.

What Parents Can Do

In addition to the other suggestions in this book, you will find it helpful to obtain as much information specific to gay teens as you can find. Find out about organizations and agencies that offer resources for gay teens and their parents in your community. The Parents and Friends of Lesbians and Gays

(P-FLAG) organization conducts support groups for parents in communities all over the United States. Gay adults you know can offer support, information, or can provide positive examples of healthy relationships or the coming out process.

It is important to reach out and ask questions, even if your teen projects an attitude that it is none of your business. In order to help, you may have to put your judgments about your teen's sexuality aside. Overcoming any negative feelings you may have about homosexuality could take time; but it is not necessary to wait for that before helping your teen become safe from violence. Whether straight, gay or bisexual, your teen needs your support to deal with a violent relationship. It is *not* helpful or effective to let negative attitudes about your teen's sexuality interfere with the support he or she needs.

Gay teens have told us that one of the hardest aspects of being in an abusive relationship has been the isolation. As Jeffrey said, having nonjudgmental people close to him who encouraged him to make healthy decisions made a difference in his getting away from his batterer.

11

FOR PARENTS OF
ABUSIVE TEENS

Nancy's Story

At first I couldn't believe it. There was a frightening similarity to what my first husband, Matt's father, did to me. Matt was definitely having a hard time. He would flare up over nothing and go slamming around the house. I heard him blow up at his girlfriend, talking mean to her on the phone. It seemed that he was calling her all the time, as if he was checking up on her. I didn't know what was going on with her or why they fought so much. I tried to talk to him about it but he shined me on, and told me to stay out of his business. This was very upsetting. I was worried about what kind of relationship he was having with this girl.

Then one day she was over and they had a big fight up in Matt's room. I heard things being thrown, and she went running out of the house. I saw that her nose was bleeding. I was furious! I was ashamed that my son could do that. I screamed at him that he was just like his father, and how dare he act that way. Matt stormed out of the house and didn't come back that night. I couldn't sleep. I didn't know what to do.

Matt could be so sweet. I had seen plenty of signs of his temper before, but I never believed he would be like his father. To tell you the truth, I was a little afraid of his temper.

My husband and I talked most of the night. He thinks I'm too easy on Matt. We decided to find someplace that Matt could get counseling, and to insist on his getting help. We sat Matt down and told him that he has a big problem. We said we'd help him but he had to help himself. At first, he refused to listen. He kept saying that his girlfriend pushed him too far. "What did she expect?!" he complained. I got so upset with him. I told him that if he wouldn't go for help, I'd call the police myself. I told him he couldn't hurt his girlfriend the way his father hurt me. I think he finally believed me.

Matt's been going to see a counselor, reluctantly. His girlfriend broke up with him, and he's depressed and moody. He thinks if he goes to a counselor she will get back with him. I told him he had better not count on it. I really don't know what's going to happen with my son. I'm still worried. He'll be eighteen soon and it will be impossible to make him do anything.

You may be reading this book because you are concerned that your son or daughter behaves abusively toward a girlfriend or boyfriend. You may suspect it, but have difficulty finding out what is really going on. You may know that your son is treating his girlfriend badly, but are not sure if what he is doing is abusive. You may know he is being abusive, but don't know what to do about it. We will continue to refer to the abuser as "he" and the abused as "she" to reflect the reality that most often young men are the batterers and most often young women are the victims.

• • •

Recognizing Abusive Behavior

Parents have learned about their teen's abusive behavior in a variety of ways. You may have heard your son on the phone with his girlfriend. He may be calling her constantly, checking up on her. He may be telling her what she can and can't do. He may be interrogating her about where she has been, who she was with, and so forth. You may overhear him becoming enraged and verbally violent on the phone—for example, calling her names, yelling, saying brutally mean things, or criticizing her.

You may have learned about your son's abusive behavior because he tells you about it. He may tell you about the time he spends with his girlfriend, or his interactions with her, and you can see that he is jealous and restrictive, or that he talks in a humiliating or degrading way about her appearance or personality. When you have conversations with him, he may seem obsessive about his girlfriend, and unable to focus on anything else. He may tell you about fights he has with his girlfriend. He may be troubled about his violence during their fights, and tell you that he has a problem and he needs help. He may be blaming his girlfriend for their fights, and it is apparent to you that he is not seeing his responsibility for their problems.

You may find out about your son's violence if you have seen him verbally or physically attacking his girlfriend, or if someone in your family, a friend or a neighbor has seen him being abusive and told you about it.

You may suspect that he is violent with his girlfriend because you have seen him being violent in other situations, for example with you, with his brother or sister, or with friends. You may suspect that he is violent with her because he generally has trouble managing his temper. You may also suspect that he is violent toward his girlfriend because he abuses drugs or alcohol, and his behavior becomes violent and mean when he is under the influence.

You may find out about your son's violence toward his girlfriend from his school, the police or some other authority. You may find out from his girlfriend or her family, who tell you because they want you to intervene to stop his violence or because they want you to keep him away from her.

For more information on signs that will help you detect abuse in a relationship, see *Chapter 2, Recognizing the Warning Signs*.

Confronting Your Teen's Abusive Behavior

When you discover that your teen is abusive or violent toward his girlfriend, your first reaction may be disbelief. He may deny it or minimize it, saying his girlfriend is lying, or that they had a fight but it wasn't that bad. He may blame her, saying that she provokes him, or that it was really she who hit him, and that he is being victimized by her. Even if he acknowledges his violence, you may not believe it if you feel that this can't be true of your child.

You can't ignore a problem like violence. You must take it seriously. If you ignore it now, during the teen years, later it will probably get worse and cause more and more harm. As difficult as this might be, you must make the decision to overcome the impulse to deny the violence, and commit to dealing with it.

If you have reason to suspect that your teen is violent or abusive, but you don't know for certain, you can try to find out. You can ask him about it, and tell him the reasons that you believe it could be true. You can ask his girlfriend. You can ask his friends or someone at school. If your son denies it, ask again, being clear about what you have seen or heard. Many teens don't use words like "battering" or "abuse." They are more likely to respond to questions about *specific* kinds of behavior, such as hitting, yelling, name-calling, or interrogating.

When you talk to your son, his girlfriend or his friends, you can tell them that this is serious, and you want to know what is going on so that you can do something about it. You can let your son know that he needs help, and that you will work with him to find out how to get the help he needs. While offering to be supportive of him as a person, and of his efforts to overcome his problems, you can let him know that you will not do anything that might lead him to believe that you support or tolerate his violence. As a parent, you may have to make the difficult decision to report your son's violence to the police, or to not protect him from being arrested if his girlfriend reports him.

If he won't listen to you or you are overwhelmed by his persistent violence or abuse, you may find it helpful to read *Chapter 5: Setting Limits* and *Chapter 6: Avoiding Power Struggles*.

Contacting the Victim of Your Teen's Abuse

If you are having trouble dealing with your son's violence, manipulations or substance abuse, then you have something in common with his girlfriend. When you make it clear to him that you will not tolerate his violence, you can also let him know that you will support anyone affected by his violence, i.e., his girlfriend. You and his girlfriend (and possibly her family) can support each other in dealing with your son's violence and help each other set limits on what you will tolerate.

A few months after her daughter Lisa started seeing

Stewart, Marilyn got a call from Stewart's mother, Amy. "You and your husband had better get over here. Stewart is a mess, on crack, yelling and waving around a metal pipe. He's got my neighbor's truck and Lisa in it, threatening her, and Lord knows where he's going to take her." Together they were able to contact the police, find Lisa and get her to safety.

Amy couldn't stop Stewart by herself, but when she involved Lisa's parents, they were all better able to handle the situation together. Lisa's parents wouldn't have known that Lisa was in trouble if Amy hadn't called. Stewart got a clear message from his mother: I will not be silent or hide this problem, and I will do whatever I can to confront your violence.

The Parent's Emotional Rollercoaster

As the parent of a violent child, you may experience the same emotional rollercoaster as the parents of a victim. You and your family may be going through ups and downs that parallel the tension and explosiveness of your son, especially if he lives with you. The relationship between spouses is often affected when parents disagree about what to do. Often one parent is protective and the other confrontational. If your family life is chaotic, your son's violence may be only one problem among many that you have to deal with. Dealing with violence can be overwhelming and confusing.

As Nancy expressed in her story at the beginning of this chapter, feelings of fear, shame and guilt are common to many parents. On discovering that their child is violent, parents have told us that they felt ashamed because they believed they caused their son's problems. They felt ashamed of having a child with such serious problems. They were afraid that their son could seriously injure or kill his girlfriend or someone else. They felt ineffective and overpowered by their child, especially if he challenged their parental authority. They felt terrible about the consequences of and the harm caused by their son's behavior.

As a parent, you're not responsible for your child's choices. Your behavior or parenting may have contributed to the difficulties your teen is now experiencing. However, many children who grew up around violence (a parent's or someone else's) have made the choice not to be violent. Growing up around violence is an issue that must be dealt with, but one can still make choices about one's behavior.

You may feel guilty because you believe that the violence is your fault. Guilt is not helpful. Once you recognize the problem and take responsibility for your part in it, you must move on and do something about it. If you become immobilized, immersed in your guilt, you will not be helpful to yourself or anyone else.

Seeking Support

Parents of abusers must reach out and get help and support from others. It is very important to break through the silence. There is an understandable reluctance to talk about the problem with others if parents expect to be judged. But there is no chance for change if parents *don't* talk about the problem. Take the risk and find friends, family members and people in your community who will actively discourage your son's violence and attitudes toward his girlfriend, and who will help you to confront his problem and provide support during his process of change.

Getting Help

The major factor in whether or not a batterer is able to overcome his abusive behavior is motivation. A teen who is horrified by his own violent behavior will make the commitment to go through the difficult process of change. Unfortunately, many abusive teens minimize and deny the seriousness of their problem. If his girlfriend breaks up with him, an abusive teen will often seek help primarily because he wants to get her back. This could result in his getting the help he needs to change, but he must make the long-term commitment to behave differently. If he only focuses on reuniting with his ex-girlfriend, the problem of violence is not addressed. If he gets sober or clean, his violent behavior may change. But teens are often violent when they are not drinking or using drugs. The underlying causes of their violence must be addressed as well as their substance abuse. Counseling can help do this.

Parents must not only help find the counseling, but, to the best of their ability, insist that their teen actually gets help. You can also influence your teen's motivation to change.

To find out about counseling resources, call your local domestic violence program hotline or teenline, a teen abuse prevention program and your district attorney's office for referrals to batterers' support groups and treatment programs.

You should also find out how the juvenile justice system in your area (or the adult justice system, if your teen is over eighteen) proceeds in teen domestic violence cases. You will then have the information you need to let your teen know about the consequences of his violent behavior.

Another strategy for getting help is informing people who should know, for example a school counselor or principal. Your aim is to have your son's abusive behavior out in the open and taken seriously, and to extend the safety net for his girlfriend.

Resources for young men who batter are scarce but expanding in the United States. There are psycho-educational and therapy groups available through domestic violence programs; recovery programs such as Alcoholics Anonymous, Alateen, and Cocaine Anonymous, which deal with substance abuse issues; school groups for students having problems in general; youth service agencies; and gang prevention services.

PARENTING FOR
HEALTHY RELATIONSHIPS

As you have been reading about the facts and the patterns of battering relationships, you may have asked yourself, "How can parents prevent this from happening? What can we do so that our children are prepared for healthy relationships? How can we teach them not to be abusive toward or to be abused by someone they love?" This chapter will be helpful if your teen is in a battering relationship, or if your teen is just beginning to date.

You have already taken the most important first step in preventing interpersonal violence: by reading this book, you are acknowledging that it happens in teen relationships. You are also finding out that it can happen in any family, not only to "other people," but to families just like your own. Denial of this reality hinders parents from preparing their children to be alert to the possibility of relationship violence.

As parents we may say, "I'll kill anyone who hurts my daughter," as if saying these words creates a circle of protection around our children. But this attitude may keep us from teaching children skills of their own that are necessary for preventing violence.

We must teach our children not only to be cautious of the danger that can come from a stranger, but also to be prepared for potential violence from someone they know. The fact is that the majority of incidents of violence against women and girls is perpetrated by acquaintances and intimates. Our daughters need to have information about abuse and how to prevent it.

For example, a teen who has learned not to get into a car with a stranger (good advice at any age) will need more complex strategies to deal with being in a car with an acquaintance who becomes violent. Violence prevention strategies for dating situations that take place in a car may involve analyzing the options available to get away to a safe place, to get help or to defend oneself physically.

The best approach to preparing children to prevent interpersonal violence is (1) to teach them to think about their own safety and (2) to teach them skills that form the basis for healthy relationships.

Teaching Your Teens to Protect Themselves

Although there is a great deal parents can do to protect children and teens from violence, it is also important to be realistic about what we cannot do. It is impossible to completely control teens' environments as they venture out into new situations. Parents can't eliminate danger, but they can help their children think about reducing the risks they take. The best safety strategies are not based on parental protectiveness or rules, but on teens' ability to think about choices and options for taking action to protect themselves. Teaching teens to be aware, alert and assertive gives them the ability to think and take action.

Awareness

Awareness is the foundation of self-protection and personal security. It involves paying attention to what is happening in a given situation, with a mind free of misconceptions.

You can start by talking to your teen about the myths and realities of dating violence. Sometimes teens—and adults—are lulled into a false sense of security: "It can't happen to me." Misconceptions and stereotypes reinforce and justify the use and tolerance of violence, and keep us from taking action to prevent or stop it. Some common misconceptions are:

- Girls like abuse or they wouldn't put up with it.
- Guys hit and yell to show their love.
- A guy has to show his girlfriend who is boss.

As you become more informed about what is true and what is not, you are able to discuss these harmful misconceptions with your teen. We recommend reading and discussing the misconceptions and realities in *Appendices A* and *B*.

There is other information in this book that you can discuss with your teen. Teens can learn the warning signs of an abusive relationship (*Chapter 2*) and the patterns that can be recognized if they occur, such as the cycle of violence (*Chapter 1*). You may suggest that your teen read *In Love and In Danger: A Teen's Guide to Breaking Free of Abusive Relationships* by Barrie Levy.

Awareness of risks and vulnerability is an important safety factor for a teen. We must empower our children to take care of themselves by getting them to think about the risks inherent in their activities and then planning for their safety. It helps to begin this process with children when they are young because as they get older, teens resist acknowledging their vulnerability to their parents.

There are many ways to do this. When your child asks for permission to go somewhere, before saying yes or no, you can ask him or her to evaluate the safety of the situation. For example, when your teen wants to go to a party, you can ask: "How are you getting there and back? If John is going to drive you back, what if he decides to drink? Then what will you do? What kind of backup plans do you have for ensuring your safety or for reacting to an emergency?" The teen is encouraged to think about his or her own safety.

Another way to teach teens to think about their safety is to brainstorm all the possible ways to handle a variety of scenarios. For example, you can ask your teen, "What if . . . ?" and describe a scenario of a situation they might encounter when out with friends, on a date with someone new, or when out with a boyfriend or girlfriend. Another way to prompt discussion is to bring up events that have actually happened, for example a news report or the experience of a neighbor or a friend. Without having a predetermined right or wrong answer, you can brainstorm together all the possibilities for handling the situation. Similar discussions can take place after seeing a movie, a television show or something your teen has seen and is curious about.

Another kind of awareness, awareness of ourselves, involves knowing what we want and don't want, what we like and don't like, what is important to us, what our values are, and what motivates us. Developing self-awareness is as important for teens as it is for adults. Parents can guide children to know themselves by talking with them about what they believe, what they care about and what they value. If we are intent on imposing our own values on our children, we hinder the process by which they learn their own values and learn to think for themselves. It is important to support teens' sense of autonomy in order to encourage them to think, choose and make decisions for themselves. They can be encouraged to think about the different ways to handle love and sexual relationships, what the consequences are of each, and how they can decide what is best for them. They need to know that they have real choices about the way they will lead their lives.

Assertiveness

Assertiveness is an important skill in preventing violence. In rape situations, for example, assertive responses have proven a successful self-defense technique in the majority of resisted assaults. Assertiveness is the ability to exercise one's own rights while respecting the rights of others. Being assertive means communicating exactly what you want and don't want, standing up for yourself, and stating your opinions, thoughts and feelings without abusing others.

Developing assertiveness skills can be as challenging for adults as it is for teens. One mother reported to us, "I realized that I would do anything to defend my children, but I could not imagine standing up for myself. I had to take a long, hard look at the values I was taught."

This mother was also referring to the values taught in a society that links assertiveness to stereotyped expectations of masculine and feminine behavior. When boys learn to behave in stereotypically masculine ways, they feel that they are supposed to be aggressive and to expect to get their way no matter how anyone else feels. When girls learn to behave in stereotypically feminine ways, they feel that they are supposed to accept what others want from them, to be passive, and that it is selfish to be direct about what they want. With these kinds of expectations, neither boys nor girls learn to be assertive.

Boys and girls must learn the differences between passive (under-assertive), aggressive and assertive behavior. Parents can help teens develop assertiveness skills by pointing out these differences, and by demonstrating assertive behavior. They can also encourage their teens to communicate assertively with family members.

Passive, or under-assertive, people make excuses for their actions and behavior and speak in a voice that is too soft or inaudible. They apologize for what they are about to say. They are afraid to say so when they disagree with someone. They can't say no when someone wants something from them. They automatically blame themselves when something goes wrong. They look away from the person they are talking to. They give mixed messages. They focus too little on their own wants and needs when with others.

Aggressive, or over-assertive, people don't allow others to speak, and act overbearing and intimidating. They yell or speak loudly. They blame others when there is a problem. In a conflict or a disagreement, they take the offensive without listening to others. They ignore the needs or wishes of others. They sometimes resort to verbal abuse or physical violence when they don't get their way.

Assertive people communicate their feelings clearly and state their opinions directly. They look directly at the other person. They give honest feedback. They give clear messages with their words as well as with their body language. They do not attempt to control or manipulate others. They accept the consequences of, and responsibility for, their assertiveness. They recognize that risk is involved in openly expressing feelings and opinions to others, and choose to behave either under-assertively, assertively or aggressively according to the particular situation.

Teens can learn to decide what is the most appropriate response in a given situation. Deciding when to be assertive is as important as knowing how to be assertive. Sometimes it may be necessary to de-escalate an explosive situation by replacing an assertive response with an underassertive one. Sometimes it may be necessary to change from an assertive stance to an aggressive one, for example to protect oneself and get away from a physically violent situation. It takes practice to develop assertiveness skills and the flexibility to use them well.

Encourage your teen to take a self-defense course to develop assertiveness skills. A good self-defense course trains people to prepare for and to think in dangerous situations. In addition to teaching safety strategies and physical self-defense techniques, it helps people to develop their awareness, to assess a situation and select options and choices.

You can practice the following technique: Ask your teen, "Have you ever said yes when you wanted to say no?" Recount some of your own experiences. Discuss how it felt afterwards, the feeling that "I should have said...." Practice with each other, describing what you might have said or done if you were given another chance in each situation. Don't worry about whether your teen comes up with the "right answer." The point is to practice articulating what you want or need effectively.

Conflict Resolution

Conflict and disagreement are normal and expected in relationships. Resolving conflicts in a manner agreeable to all parties involves special skills. Practicing conflict resolution and problem-solving in your family teaches these skills to your teen, who can apply them to other situations outside your home. When parents provide models of effective interpersonal interactions, they are teaching violence prevention skills. If you feel you aren't able to provide models of these skills, you can find other ways for your teen to learn them, such as through classes or groups.

Productive confrontation involves honest communication, willingness to listen to others, assertiveness, compromise and problem-solving. You can teach your children this five-step technique for problem-solving:

1. Discuss and define the problem from each person's point of view (by listening and communicating clearly).

Jane: "I want to spend Christmas Day with you, and I want you to come to my house."

John: "But I want to spend it with my family."

Jane: "The problem is we both want to be together on Christmas and we both want to be with our families, too."

2. Brainstorm possible solutions.

John: "We can go to my family's house this year and to yours next year."

Jane: "I can go to my family's and you can go to yours."

John: "We can spend half the day with each."

Jane: "We can spend the day by ourselves and avoid the whole thing."

3. Evaluate and choose a solution that is acceptable to both people (by negotiating).

John: "We can't go to your family's house and not mine because my family will be too upset and I can't deal with that."

Jane: "The same is true for my family."

John: "So . . . we can't avoid our families, and I really want to be with you."

Jane: "Let's split the day between our two families, or go to your family's house on Christmas Eve and to mine on Christmas Day."

John: "OK. Let's go to my family's on Christmas Eve and to yours on Christmas Day."

4. Implement the solution that has been negotiated.

5. Evaluate the outcome at a later date.

John: "I'm glad we saw both our families the way we did, but my mother didn't like it that I wasn't there for Christmas dinner."

Jane: "This worked out just fine for me."

John: "Maybe next year or for Easter we'll have the holiday dinner with my family."

Changing Values and Attitudes

Parents have another role to play in violence prevention. We must challenge the attitudes and institutions within our own cultures and communities that create and sustain a tolerance for violence in intimate relationships and in general.

You may be aware of the extent to which your children are exposed to justifications for violence. We are all surrounded by images of violence: in our neighborhoods, in movies, on television. Sometimes the images are terrifying, but too often they glorify or justify violence. It is accepted as a way to resolve conflicts and as a means to retaliate against wrongdoing. "He made me so mad, I hit him." "They started it but I finished it." These statements are heard about peers, and, in different words, about countries at war.

Parents can prevent violence by challenging these mistaken ideas and the damaging images of "justified" violence. When you recognize the presence of these attitudes, you can speak up. If you do not, violence in relationships remains invisible, tolerated and accepted. So many girls have told us that when they were hit by their boyfriends in school or in a public place such as a mall, people walked by and said nothing. Both the boy and girl then believed there was nothing wrong with the boyfriend's behavior. Silence reinforces the impression among teens that violence in relationships is normal.

Every day in your family life there are opportunities to challenge mistaken assumptions about violence. You can help your children critique what they see in the media. You can discuss alternatives to what they see. You can repeatedly assert that no one deserves to be emotionally, verbally or physically abused, and that violence is never justified. You may find you have to confront some of your own values and attitudes. We must all learn to expand our awareness of the messages about violence that surround us.

Teaching Teens About Healthy Relationships

The teen years are a time of exploring and learning about relationships. Teens often don't know what constitutes a healthy relationship, or have not defined what this means to them personally.

You can encourage your children to think about their relationships, present and future, by talking to them about healthy relationships, pointing out features of good relationships when they are around them or see them in books or movies, and opening a dialogue in which they think about what they look for in a boyfriend or girlfriend. To identify the differences between relationships that are built on respect and those that are not, describe examples from your own experience. Support them for thinking for themselves if they express an opinion different from yours.

In addition to feelings of love, passion, affection, shared likes and dislikes, and enjoying time together, emphasize the following characteristics of healthy relationships with your teen:

- Both partners give and take, each getting their way some of the time and compromising some of the time.
- They respect each other, and value one another's opinions.
- They support and encourage one another's goals and ambitions.
- They trust one another, and learn not to inflict jealous and restrictive feelings on the other if they should arise.
- Neither is afraid of the other.
- They communicate openly and honestly, and make their partners feel safe in expressing themselves.
- They share responsibility in decisionmaking.
- They accept the differences between them.
- They encourage each other to have friends and activities outside the relationship.

Of course, experience is the best teacher, but parents can help teens develop their own ideas and good judgment about what is healthy for them. Parents can't prevent broken hearts from failed relationships, but they can help their teens want what is healthy and positive, and to seek it in all areas of their lives, including relationships.

Violence prevention measures can be implemented in a multitude of ways and settings. Skills for healthy relationships can be encouraged and learned from many different sources, including friends, school, media and families. As parents we can be a tremendous resource for our teens when we are aware and informed, foster good self-esteem, encourage assertiveness, talk about sensitive and volatile issues with teens, empower them, communicate openly with them and respect their ideas and feelings.

13

HEALING

There is so much for parents to be prepared for and to handle in the lives of our teenagers. Who expected to have to deal with hidden violence or abuse in our teenagers' relationships? Domestic violence is a reality affecting many families, and most of us are unprepared to deal with it. Whether you have experienced it directly or are learning about it so that you can help your teen prevent it, once you know about this kind of fear and challenge, you have been changed.

Everyone who has been through domestic violence has been profoundly affected by it. They go on, one way or another, but relationships, priorities, the ability to cope, ways of seeing other people are often changed. How can a family *not* be affected, for example, when a child of the batterer is now part of the family, or when family members have lived with threats of being killed, or when parents' tension wreaks havoc on their marriage? Families can be brought closer together or torn apart. Dating violence is a serious business that can affect an entire family, testing the strengths and exacerbating the weaknesses of each individual family member and the family as a whole.

For a while after the battering relationship has ended, you may feel afraid that your daughter will see or get involved with the batterer again. As you know, many girls try to break up several times before finally ending the relationship. The point is that breaking up is possible. The more time that goes by, and the more actively your family and your daughter rebuild your strengths, the calmer you will become about this.

Similarly, you may fear that your teen will be in a violent relationship again in the future. The reality is that most teens become acutely aware of the warning signs of abuse after having been through it, and stay away from anyone who might be like their batterer. Others, especially if they have not gone through a process to understand the battering experience, may be attracted to someone else who becomes abusive. You won't know for a while, but you can support your teen's dealing with the emotional effects of the battering, and thereby reduce the risk of another similar experience.

Many parents feel they are no longer able to believe or trust their teens after realizing how many lies have been told to cover up the abuse and/or the relationship itself. You may also find that you are over-protective or hyper-vigilant long after your teen is out of danger, as it takes time to heal.

Healing involves rebuilding trust between parents and teens, and between the parents themselves who may have become disconnected from each other because of differences in their reactions to their daughter's situation.

One of the results of dating violence is that you and your teen have missed out on some of the usual experiences of adolescence, and now need to fill in the developmental gaps. Some teens feel they have to make up for the missed social life and academic accomplishments of high school. As a parent, you may find yourself dealing with a fifteen-year-old's issues with your nineteen-year-old.

You may find that your confidence as a parent has been shaken, as well as your confidence in your teen's capabilities, choices and resiliency. Certainly, your sense of safety and security has been threatened. You will find it returns slowly.

Doing your best as a parent means finding the balance between actively participating in your teens' life and accepting that you can't control them, the outcome of their choices or even what they learn from their experiences. Active participation means doing everything you can to teach, guide, influence, be a resource and support healthy choices and healing.

Families can and do heal from the ups and downs, the rollercoasters of violent relationships. Healing is a process for the whole family and takes time and attention. Healing involves managing and living with the new realities that the aftermath of a crisis brings. Healing is a time of rebuilding trust, confidence and a sense of security. The healing process involves catching up on aspects of your lives that have been neglected or interrupted.

Healing goes beyond surviving crises. It allows the family to thrive, to feel a sense of strength, from having overcome the effects of the crisis. As a parent who has supported a teen through a violent relationship, you will need to use the strengths, patience and resources you have drawn upon to continue your support for your teen and for yourself during the healing process.

Through the stories in this book, you have been introduced to families who have been profoundly affected by teen dating violence. You have benefitted from what they have learned from their experiences. Real-life stories about dating violence don't have neat conclusions. The healing process takes time. Sometimes months or years pass after the violence has ended before you fully realize its effect and the subsequent growth, building and rebuilding that has taken place. In the epilogues that follow, we revisit Margaret, Victor and Barbara. Their stories continue.

Margaret's Story

Margaret's nineteen-year-old daughter Molly and her boyfriend William broke up after a particularly violent episode, and then she discovered she was pregnant. She decided to have the baby and to give William another chance, feeling differently about him now that he was the father of her child. However, their relationship continued to deteriorate as his drinking and violence got worse.

The turning point for Molly was after she left William again and was staying with her parents, and he came by to see the baby. Molly didn't feel she could deprive him of this right. He took the baby to the park, but disappeared until the early hours of the morning. When he brought the baby back, he was drunk. The baby was hungry and dirty. Margaret's whole family was up half the night, frightened. Margaret feels Molly became closer to the family that day and that night because they all shared the experience of terror that something had happened to the baby. Margaret feels she will be dealing with the results of this relationship forever because William is the father of her grandchild. She helped Molly get custody of the baby and place restrictions on William's visitation rights. Molly is still dealing with her emotional attachment to William. Because of this, Margaret continues to have some degree of fear because William is still around. She is pleased, however, that Molly has been attending a support group for battered women. She has returned to school, is doing well and is making plans for her future as a nurse.

Occasionally Margaret still has to be a buffer between Frank, her husband, and Molly as he continues to struggle with his anger towards William. Frank has become totally attached to the baby. Molly's brothers also feel protective of the baby. Under pressure from Margaret, they have come to terms with the fact that William is in their lives, and they are resigned to keeping their anger under control. Otherwise they don't get too involved with Molly, having grown fed up with her situation.

Molly's younger sister is still a confidante, and often gets caught up in the drama of her sister's life. But as she is getting older, she has a busy social life and is gradually becoming less involved with Molly's.

Although it is sometimes a strain, Margaret feels she has been effective in her central role in the family. She wishes Molly had never met William. But she has come to accept that Molly makes her own choices, and that the family has to live with that. Margaret also expects Molly to accept that people in her family all have to live their lives too.

Victor's Story

Fifteen-year-old Emilia tried to slow things down with Thomas, who was much older (twenty-three). Thomas became increasingly emotionally controlling, isolating her more and more. Victor and Rosa pressured her to break up with him, but she became more secretive about the relationship. She still allowed her family to convince her to spend time with them. Her stepfather Victor's persistent demonstration of his concern for her was a new experience after years of not having a father around.

One day she didn't come home. Terrified, Victor and Rosa went over to Thomas' house to find her. Thomas' parents insisted that Emilia had to go with Victor and Rosa. After that, she resisted Thomas' controlling behavior more, and began to assert herself with him. He became more violent, and Victor and Rosa called the police on several occasions. After going to court, Emilia began to realize the seriousness of her situation, and gradually decided that this was not what she wanted. A year later, after two attempts, she finally broke up with him.

Emilia's relationship with Thomas put a lot of strain on Victor's and Rosa's relatively new relationship. Rosa became depressed. Victor would become impatient to take action and Rosa would become immobilized. The effects of Emilia's relationship on the family at times seemed relentless.

Naturally, Victor and Rosa were facing other problems besides Emilia's boyfriend. But dealing with Emilia's abusive relationship wore them out. At one point they talked about divorce, but they continued to work at maintaining as normal a family life as possible. They were able to get through it, and were relieved when Emilia finally got away from Thomas. A solid relationship developed between Victor and his stepchildren, especially Emilia, because of everything they went through together.

Barbara's Story

Barbara maintained strong ties with her seventeen-year-old daughter Tanisha throughout Tanisha's battering relationship with Tyrone. In spite of the abuse, Tanisha thought she and Tyrone would get married. She was annoyed when Tyrone stalled by making excuses. She eventually found out from a friend that he had been seeing someone else for almost a year. He had been lying to her. Tanisha was still "hooked," believing he would get rid of the other girl and marry her because she was "the one who really understands him." Then she saw them together. She was so hurt and angry, but she realized he was lying to her about leaving the other girl. She broke up with him for the last time, no longer believing him when he tried to persuade her that he would be faithful to her.

Tanisha leaned on her family for support, knowing she would need it, as she was determined to stay away from Tyrone. Her family talked and planned together, as they had throughout the battering relationship. Her uncle, who hadn't spoken to her for a year, started talking to her again.

Barbara prayed a lot, and was glad she had a strong connection with her church and her family. Tanisha was successful at her job, which helped her self-confidence to grow outside the battering relationship. With Barbara's encouragement, Tanisha saw a counselor.

Barbara always knew she couldn't make Tanisha do what she wasn't ready to do, and kept her faith that her daughter would eventually come to her senses. When it was over, she was distressed that Tanisha had not left because of Tyrone's violence, and might have married him. She realized that although she had a lot of faith in Tanisha, she had experienced constant worry and fear that something terrible would happen to her before she got completely away from Tyrone.

Conclusion

As you finish reading this book, you have attained a great deal of information that can help you prevent or intervene to stop dating violence. You are now more prepared, knowing what to look for, what to expect and what to do. Learning as much as you can, seeking support and knowing you are not alone makes a difference. Remember, in spite of heartbreak and pain, teens recover and families are resilient. Your resilience enables you to draw upon your reserves to find the strength and capability to handle one of the most difficult problems a parent can face.

TEEN DATING VIOLENCE FACTS

Misconception: "Abuse in teen relationships is not that common or serious."

Reality: Surveys show that violence is experienced in 28% of teen relationships, and according to the FBI, 20% of homicide victims are between the ages of 15 and 24. One out of three women murdered in the U.S. is killed by a husband or boyfriend.

Productive Thinking: *"Battering is not just an adult problem; it happens with teens also and we have to become more aware of the realities of relationship violence among young people."*

Misconception: "Girls like the abuse or else they wouldn't put up with it."

Reality: Young women and girls stay in abusive relationships for a number of complex reasons, none of which include liking the abuse.

Productive Thinking: *"I have to recognize that no one stays in an abusive relationship because they like the abuse, but that leaving the relationship may be difficult."*

Misconception: "Guys yell and hit to show how much they care about their partners."

Reality: Guys yell and hit because they are using violence to try and control another person and/or are unable to control their own behavior.

Productive Thinking: *"The positive way of showing care for my partner is through understanding and respect and not violently or abusively acting out my emotions."*

Misconception: "A guy has the right to discipline his girlfriend to show her who's boss."

Reality: Discipline is used to exercise authority, such as a parent has over a child or a superior over subordinates. Unfortunately, many societies have taught and encouraged men to dominate women under the guise of discipline.

Productive Thinking: *"I do not have the right to try and control my girlfriend's or my boyfriend's behavior. The only person I have control over is myself. If I want to have a good, healthy relationship, I need to develop respect for my partner."*

Misconception: "Alcohol and/or drugs are what cause people to become violent or abusive."

Reality: Chemical substances are not the cause of violence but may act as enablers to violence by lowering inhibitions.

Productive Thinking: *"I realize that using alcohol may put me at risk for being a victim of rape, or enable me to be a perpetrator of violence."*

Misconception: "Violence only happens between people who are poor or members of a minority."

Reality: Abuse in relationships exists among all classes, races, and cultural groups in society. It even happens within same-gender relationships.

Productive Thinking: *"An abusive relationship can happen to anyone; we are not exempt because we belong to a particular group. Beliefs about other groups may stem from racism."*

Misconception: "Guys who batter are psycho-crazies."

Reality: Batterers are "normal" people that we encounter in everyday life. They can be the smartest, quietest, coolest, or the best athlete on campus. What they have in common is their inability to control their anger and aggressive impulses.

Productive Thinking: *"I cannot recognize batterers by how they look or act in public, but by how they behave in a relationship over a period of time."*

TEEN SEXUAL ASSAULT FACTS

Misconception: "Rape only happens to adults."

Reality: According to *Rape In America: A Report to the Nation*, it was found that "... rape in America is a tragedy of youth, with the majority of rape cases occurring during childhood and adolescence." Twenty-nine percent of victims were younger than 11, 32% were between the ages of 11-17, and 22% were 18-24.

Productive Thinking: *"Sexual assault can happen to anyone of any age and to both females and males. By raising my awareness, I have taken a positive step toward preventing it from happening to me."*

Misconception: "Most rapes occur as a spur-of-the-moment act in a dark alley by a stranger."

Reality: About 82% of rapes are wholly or partially planned. Seventy-five percent of females in one study and 78% of rape victims in another were assaulted by someone they knew. This includes boyfriends and husbands.

Productive Thinking: *"I realize that in addition to being aware of strangers, I must recognize that people I know may pose a potential threat to me as well. With education on assault and abuse, I can watch for signs that may place me at risk."*

Misconception: "Most rapes are inter-racial."

Reality: Rapists and their victims are likely to be of the same race (7 out of 10 for white victims; 8 out of 10 for black).

Productive Thinking: *"I realize that there are incidents of inter-racial sexual assault, but to say that most of them are may be based more on racism than fact."*

Misconception: "Rapes take place at night in unfamiliar territory."

Reality: According to the FBI, 36% of reported assaults occurred in or around the home of the victim. Other locations included commercial buildings, schools, parking lots, garages, and parks.

Additionally, 34% occurred in broad daylight.

Productive Thinking: *"By recognizing that an assault may take place at any time or any place, I can learn ways to be more secure in different locations to lower my risk of assault."*

Misconception: "Rape is just rough or bad sex. What's the big deal?"

Reality: Almost half (49%) of the survivors were fearful of serious injury or death during a rape. Rape is a violent assault that is acted out sexually and affects an individual's sense of safety and control. Rape victims are nine times more likely than victims of other crimes to attempt suicide.

Productive Thinking: *"Even though rape is acted out sexually, I must remember that it is a violation and is about power and control. It has potentially life changing effects and should be taken very seriously."*

Misconception: "The rapist is someone who is sexually unfulfilled or can't get sex."

Reality: According to a New Jersey prison study, *all* of the rapists studied had available sexual relationships at the time of the rape.

Productive Thinking: *"Sexual fulfillment is not the entire motivation for sexual assault. It is a need to exert power and control over another."*

Misconception: "Girls ask for it by the way they dress or act."

Reality: "Provocative behavior" is usually defined by a male standard. In Victorian times, showing the ankle was considered provocative.

Productive Thinking: *"Dressing in attractive ways or indicating to someone that you like them is not an invitation to be sexually violated."*

Misconception: "It's okay for a guy to force a girl to have sex with her if she makes him excited."

Reality: This attitude suggests that guys are not capable of controlling their sexual urges and it is a girl's fault if a guy cannot do so.

Productive Thinking: *"If I engage in sexual intimacy, I cannot force or coerce my partner into doing anything, and I must take responsibility for my own actions. If I choose not to participate, my partner's sexual urges are not my responsibility."*

Misconception: "It's okay for a guy to force a girl to have sex with her if he pays for everything on a date."

Reality: This attitude suggests that dating is an exchange of sex for money. On the streets this is known as prostitution. It further suggests guys plan on having sex with their dates whether their dates want to or not—planned rapes.

Productive Thinking: *"Since there are both males and females who think this way, I might want to discuss who's paying and what it means before we go out."*

Misconception: "Girls only cry rape to get back at a guy they are mad at."

Reality: Only about 2.5% of all rape charges are determined to be false—the same percentage as other felonies. As a matter of fact, it is estimated that as many as 85% of all rapes go unreported.

Productive Thinking: *"Because of the way society treats rape victims, most people would not put themselves in a position to be ridiculed, demeaned, and subject to public scrutiny if it were not true."*

Teen Dating Violence Facts and *Teen Sexual Assault Facts* are reprinted with permission from the Los Angeles Commission on Assaults Against Women, *In Touch with Teens: A Teen Relationship Violence Curriculum.*

NOTES

Chapter One

1. D. Sugarman and G. Hotaling (1991). "Dating Violence: A Review of Contextual and Risk Factors." In B. Levy, Ed., *Dating Violence: Young Women in Danger*. Seattle: Seal Press. Pp. 100-118.
2. S. Ageton (1983). *Sexual Assault Among Adolescents*. Lexington, MA: Heath.
3. U.S. Federal Bureau of Investigation (1989). Uniform Crime Reports. Washington, D.C.: Author.
4. FBI, op. cit.
5. Sugarman and Hotaling, op. cit.

Chapter Two

1. D. Graham and E. Rawlings (1991). "Bonding With Abusive Dating Partners: Dynamics of Stockholm Syndrome." In B. Levy, Ed., *Dating Violence: Young Women in Danger*. Seattle: Seal Press. Pp. 119-135.

Chapter Five

1. T. Gordon (1970), *Parent Effectiveness Training*. New York: Peter Wyden, Inc. Pp. 37-39.

Chapter Six

1. T. Gordon (1979). *Parent Effectiveness Training*. New York: Peter H. Wyden, Inc. Pp. 48.
2. T. Gordon, *op. cit.*, pp. 155.
3. Alcoholics Anonymous World Services (1952). "Step Three." *Twelve Steps and Twelve Traditions*. New York: Author. Pp. 41.

Chapter Seven

1. L. Prato and R. Braham (1991). "Coordinating a Community Response to Teen Dating Violence." In B. Levy, ed., *Dating Violence: Young Women in Danger*. Seattle: Seal Press. Pp. 153-163.

Chapter Eight

1. S. Kuehl (1991). "Legal Remedies for Teen Dating Violence." In B. Levy (Ed.), *Dating Violence: Young Women in Danger*. Seattle: Seal Press. Pp. 209-210.
2. This section is adapted from S. Kuehl, *op. cit.*

INDEX

controlling behavior, 5, 7-8, 19, 76-79
cooperation of victim, 84
counseling, 27, 55, 99-101, 102-106, 138-140
criminal harassment, 112
criminal law system, 111-117. *See also* civil law system; legal system; police involvement
cultural excuses for behavior, 121-122
cultural values, 118-124, 145-146, 149-150
cycle of violence, 11-16, 37-38, 101. *See also* patterns of violence
date rape, 3, 22-27, 31, 161-165. *See also* abuse; sexual assault; violence
dating and cultural values, 118-119
dating violence, 143, 161-162
dependency and addictive relationships, 39-40
depression, 12, 21-22, 98
domestic violence shelters, 96, 103-104, 139
drug abuse, 22, 33-34, 40-41, 80, 99. *See also* Alateen; Alcoholics Anonymous; Cocaine Anonymous
effect of abusive relationships on parents and siblings, 44-47, 52, 55-63, 153-160
effective listening, 71-73. *See also* listening
emotional abuse, 6-8, 10, 19-20. *See also* verbal abuse; violence
emotional impact
of breaking up, 97-99
on parents, 44-46, 55-63, 69, 74, 78-79, 137-138, 153-160
on siblings, 46-47, 52, 153-160
endangerment, reckless, 112
ending abusive relationships, 4
ethnic traditions, 118-124
excuses for behavior, 15, 20-21
cultural, 121-122

family
relationships within, 153-160
support of, 85, 87-91
family of abuser, support of, 89-90
fear, 18, 32-33, 35-37
feelings
of parents, 44-46, 55-63, 69, 74, 78-79, 137-138, 153-160
of siblings, 46-47, 52, 153-160
friends, support of, 53, 75, 85, 87-91
gay relationships, 125-131
gender
roles, 30-31, 119, 120-121, 145-146
and violence, 4
Gordon, Thomas, 70
groups, support, 103-104, 139-140
guardian ad litem, 112
harassment, 91-93, 109
criminal, 112
health clinics, 104-105
healthy relationships, 150-151
homicide statistics, 4
homophobia, 127, 130-131
homosexual relationships, 125-131
Hostage Syndrome, 38-39
hotlines, 103, 139
In Love and In Danger, 143
influence of parents, 79-80
influences, cultural, 118-124
injuries, unexplained, 17-18
insecurity, 30, 32-33
isolation, 8, 21-22, 68-69, 127, 129-131
jealousy, 7, 21, 29-30
Jewish culture, 119
law. *See* civil law system; criminal law system; legal system; police involvement
legal system, 111-117, 139. *See also* police involvement
lesbian relationships, 125-131
limits, setting, 55-57
listening, 52-54, 71-73, 82
loss, fear of, 32-33

love, romantic, 37-38, 39-40
marriage, 118, 121
minors, rights of, 112
misconceptions about dating violence, 143
mothers, teen, 97
murder statistics, 4
myths about dating violence, 143
need for control, compulsive, 32-33
neighbors, support of, 90-91
nurturing relationships, 40
oppression, cultural, 119
Parent Effectiveness Training, 70
parents
    anger, managing, 58-63, 69
    of batterer, 132-140
    conflicts between, 62-63
    effects of abusive relationships on, 44-46, 54-63, 69, 74, 137-138, 153-160
        homophobia, 127, 130-131
        influence, 79-80
        as resources, 79-80
        respect of, 66-68
        support for, 54-55, 59-60, 138
        support of, 26-27, 46, 75, 85, 87-91, 98-99, 141-152, 153-160
        supporting siblings, 52
Parents and Friends of Lesbians and Gays (P-FLAG), 130-131
passive behavior, 145-147
passive listening, 52-54
patterns of violence, 84, 85. *See also* cycle of violence
peer pressure, 30-31
physical abuse, 8-9, 10. *See also* abuse; date rape; sexual assault; physical violence; violence
physical violence, 21, 161-165. *See also* abuse; date rape; sexual assault; violence
    and gender, 4
    increasing severity of, 68-69
    onset of, 4
    statistics, 3-4, 161-162, 163-165

tolerance of, 4-5
Planned Parenthood, 109
planning for safety issues, 85-87
police involvement, 54, 84, 95, 112-117, 139. *See also* civil law system; criminal law system; legal system
possessiveness, 7
power, asserting, 30
power struggles, 76-79, 80-82
powerlessness, 25
pressure, peer, 30-31
preventing violence, 141-152
protection, self, 142-149
racism, 119
rape, date, 3, 22-27, 31, 161-165. *See also* abuse; sexual assault;violence
rape, definition of, 23-24
Rape Trauma Syndrome, 25-26
relationships
    addictive, 39-40
    bisexual, 125-131
    closeted, 127, 129
    gay, 125-131
    healthy, 141-152
    lesbian, 125-131
    nurturing, 40
    qualities of healthy, 150-151
    within family, 153-160
relationships, abusive
    ending, 4
    parents, effects on , 44-46, 55-63, 153-160
    reasons for staying in, 34-41
    siblings, effects on , 46-47, 52, 153-160
religious
    beliefs, 118-124
    communities, 105
resolving conflicts, 147-149
resources, 54, 83-84, 130-131, 138-140
    counseling, 27, 55, 99-101, 102-106, 138-140
    legal system, 111-117, 139

ABOUT THE AUTHORS

Barrie Levy, M.S.W., is the author of *Skills for Violence-Free Relationships: Curriculum for Young People* and *In Love and In Danger: A Teen's Guide to Breaking Free of Abusive Relationships*, and the editor of *Dating Violence: Young Women in Danger*. She has been involved in the movement against violence against women for twenty years. She lives in Los Angeles, California, where she works as a psychotherapist, consultant and trainer, and teaches at the School of Social Welfare, University of California, Los Angeles.

Patricia Occhiuzzo Giggans, M.A., is the Executive Director of the Los Angeles Commission on Assaults Against Women (LACAAW), a sexual assault, domestic violence, and child abuse prevention center. She co-authored LACAAW's *In Touch with Teens: A Teen Relationship Violence Curriculum* and LACAAW's *Women's Self-Defense: The Complete Guide to Assault Prevention*. She a Master Self-Defense Trainer and has worked in the field of violence prevention for more than twenty years.

SELECTED TITLES FROM SEAL PRESS

IN LOVE AND IN DANGER: *A Teen's Guide to Breaking Free of Abusive Relationships* by Barrie Levy. $8.95, 1-878067-26-5. A book for teenagers about how to recognize abusive dating relationships and how to find help.

DATING VIOLENCE: *Young Women in Danger* edited by Barrie Levy. $16.95. 1-878067-03-6. A comprehensive resource addressing the problem of teen dating violence.

GETTING FREE: *You Can End Abuse and Take Back Your Life* by Ginny NiCarthy. $12.95, 0-931188-37-7. A self-help book for battered women.

GETTING FREE: *Are You Abused? (And What to Do About It)* narrated by Ginny NiCarthy. Audiocassette, 60 minutes. $10.95, 0-931188-84-9. Based on the book.

YOU CAN BE FREE: *An Easy-to-Read Handbook for Abused Women* by Ginny NiCarthy and Sue Davidson. $6.95, 0-931188-68-7.

THE ONES WHO GOT AWAY: *Women Who Left Abusive Partners* by Ginny NiCarthy. $11.95, 0-931188-49-0.

A COMMUNITY SECRET: *For the Filipina in an Abusive Relationship* by Jacqueline Agtuca, in collaboration with The Asian Women's Shelter. $5.95, 1-878067-44-3. Written in easy-to-read English.

CHAIN CHAIN CHANGE: *For Black Women in Abusive Relationships*, expanded second edition, by Evelyn C. White. $8.95, 1-878067-60-5. Support and information for African-American women.

MEJOR SOLA QUE MAL ACOMPAÑADA: *For the Latina in an Abusive Relationship/Para la Mujer Golpeada* by Myrna M. Zambrano. $10.95, 0-931188-26-1. A bilingual handbook in Spanish and English.

¡No Más!: *Guía para la mujer golpeada* by Myrna M. Zambrano. $5.95, 1-878067-50-8. A simplified version of *Mejor Sola Que Mal Acompañada*, in Spanish.

MOMMY AND DADDY ARE FIGHTING: *A Book for Children About Family Violence* by Susan Paris. $8.95, 0-931188-33-4. Illustrated by Gail Labinski.

NAMING THE VIOLENCE: *Speaking Out Against Lesbian Battering* edited by Kerry Lobel. $12.95, 0-931188-42-3.

THE SINGLE MOTHER'S COMPANION: *Essays and Stories by Women*, edited by Marsha R. Leslie. $12.95, 1-878067-56-7.

The *Women Who Dared Series* by Sue Davidson is a line of multicultural biographies that profile outstanding American women. The books are written for young adults and adult new readers. GETTING THE REAL STORY: *Nellie Bly and Ida B. Wells*. $8.95, 1-878067-16-8. Explores the lives of two pioneering women journalists. A HEART IN POLITICS: *Jeannette Rankin and Patsy T. Mink*. $9.95, 1-878067-53-2. Jeannette Rankin was the first woman elected to the United States Congress; Patsy T. Mink was the first Asian-American woman elected to Congress.

NO MORE SECRETS by Nina Weinstein. $8.95, 1-878067-00-1. A coming-of-age story that tells of sixteen-year-old Mandy's recovery from a childhood rape.

SEAL PRESS publishes many feminist books under the categories of women's studies, fiction & poetry, mysteries, health, self-help & recovery and women in sports & the outdoors. To receive a free catalog or to order directly, write to us at 3131 Western Avenue, Suite 410, Seattle, Washington 98121. Please include 16.5% of total book order for shipping and handling.